Warwickshire's
Centenary Way

described by Geoff Allen & John Roberts

****
WALKWAYS
J S Roberts
8 Hillside Close, Bartley Green
Birmingham B32 4LT
****

WARWICKSHIRE'S CENTENARY WAY

described by Geoff Allen & John Roberts.

ISBN   0 947708 33 2

First Published 1996

The Authors

GEOFF ALLEN was born in the Black Country and has been boringly static ever since. He started rambling just forty years ago, with an abortive sally from Henley in Arden, and has worn out umpteen pairs of assorted footwear, though not himself, tramping about Britain and abroad.

Since 1980 he has written a weekly walk column for the *Birmingham Evening Mail*, and has contributed to several outdoor magazines; *TGO, Country Walking* and *Rambling Today*, in addition to publishing several books of walks. He used to have a real job, working in insurance, but seized the first opportunity of early retirement.

JOHN ROBERTS was born many years ago on the Wirral. His early playgrounds were the Cheshire woods and lanes, but natural idleness delayed any real walking until he moved to the Midlands.

Over the last 25 years he has managed to shuffle round quite a lot, and written many books of walks. You will be shocked to hear that John, also, worked in insurance, and served time as a Loss Adjuster, before a spell of lecturing. He is now a full time writer and publisher with his WALKWAYS and QuercuS imprints.

Edge Hill; much nicer than pictures of Geoff and John

Contents

Introducing the
Centenary Way

At one minute past midnight on the first Saturday of 1991, five lads from the Atherstone District Scout Fellowship set out to walk through Warwickshire from Kingsbury Water Park to Upper Quinton, following a winding trail of almost 100 miles. On the following Monday at 4.58 pm three of them finished after a weekend, as their account put it, *"of fierce storms and lashing rain."*

Having achieved the first recorded continuous trek along the Centenary Way, which was not to be officially opened for another six months, the scouts admitted that their assault was *"not the best way of seeing Warwickshire."*

This guide is for those who want to tackle the walk in quite a different way. You can go at your own pace and perhaps not continuously, you can look at the landscape and absorb the experience. We have provided complete and careful guidance to the route and, we hope, enough information about the landscape and places to make your journey memorable.

But what is this Centenary Way, and where is it leading you? To quote the body that created and maintains it, it is

> *" .... a recreational footpath established by Warwickshire County Council to celebrate its 100th aniversary in 1989. It reflects the great variety of the county; its history, culture, landscape and nature. Following public footpaths, bridleways, canal towpaths and disused railways, it passes through some beautiful countryside and peaceful villages, by ancient woodland and winding streams; it reveals the immense changes that have taken place in the last century."*

The route was planned and marked out by Keith Whitton, working for the County Council on a three year contract funded by the Countryside Commission. Much of the work - building stiles and bridges, clearing vegetation - was done by volunteers and supported by Millet Leisure. The Centenary Way was officially opened by Sir John Johnson, then Chairman of the Commission, on 13th July 1991 at Upper Quinton, where it meets the Heart of England Way.

The County Council divided the Centenary Way into eleven sections and published a leaflet for each. They give information on points of interest and an outline description of the route with maps, and we must acknowledge them as the source of some of our background information. However, this book is the first "step by step" guide that can be used in either direction. We had the cooperation of the County Council in writing it, but it is independent.

We think this is helpful both to walkers and the County Council. Whilst we generally agree with their rollicking hyperbole quoted above, details of the route have been criticised, and our detached position allows us to offer improvements. Some walking on roads is inevitable on all long distance footpaths, but the southern part of the Centenary Way too often takes to the tarmac when footpaths are available. We have described the official route but offered several variations that radically reduce road walking.

The route has also been criticised on the grounds that it winds far too much in order to visit Warwickshire's three showpiece towns, Kenilworth, Warwick and Leamington Spa. We think this is misplaced. Unlike the Heart of England Way which has the objective of travel between Cannock Chase and the Cotswolds, the Centenary Way is a tour around the County and a celebration of some of its best features. On the whole, given the improvements we offer, we think you will find it absorbing and rewarding.

The Way it Goes

It seems curious that a walk through Shakespeare's county should shun its most popular area, the Forest of Arden, which has some of the best landscape, and go nowhere near Stratford upon Avon. But the route of the Centenary Way must be seen beside the older Heart of England Way, which it joins at both ends. On its journey from Staffordshire to the Cotswolds the HoEW passes down the west side of Warwickshire, via Kingsbury Water Park, Meriden, Henley in Arden, Alcester and Upper Quinton. Just to mark its outline on a map of the county prompts the idea of an eastern counterpart, so the HoEW both promotes the idea of the CW and suggests its course.

Much of the route of the Centenary Way could be called "Unknown Warwickshire"; it finds some surprisingly lonely and little known places. Starting close to the Staffordshire border in Warwickshire's "Lake District" at Kingsbury Water Park ("Fen Country" would be more appropriate), you pass Shustoke and its reservoirs and soon find yourself in the quiet countryside near Furnace End, heading for the high ground of Hartshill Hayes Country Park.

Turning south from the Hayes over a pleasantly undulating landscape, you visit Ansley, Robinson's End and Seeswood Pool, and pass Arbury Hall. The Way is briefly entangled with the industrial fringes of Bedworth, but escapes quickly and elegantly on part of Nuneaton Borough's admirable path system, "Your Green Track", to join the Coventry Canal. To quote the Way's pioneer, Keith Whitton, in the Warwickshire RA newsletter, perhaps apologising more than necessary for a couple of half miles of industrial estate:

> *" The route does not try to avoid the industrial parts in the north of the County, but shows how devastated land can be reclaimed by nature, with help from man. "*

(3)

Canal buffs will love the long miles of towpath walking that follow; Hawkesbury Junction where the Coventry Canal meets the Oxford is the highlight, a modest cluster of unpretentious brick canal buildings.

The Way swings east of Coventry via the canalside village of Ansty, and then west to visit Coombe Abbey Country Park. Here we offer an alternative route through Brinklow. Entering central Warwickshire and the Avon Valley, the route runs through a succession of pleasant villages: Brandon, Wolston, Ryton on Dunsmore, Bubbenhall and Stoneleigh. Walkers may then become tourists for a while to sample Kenilworth, Warwick and Leamington Spa.

A walk by the Grand Union Canal follows, then lonely field-paths through the Feldon, the area of Warwickshire south of the Avon. After Ufton and Harbury, hills rise ahead. Those shaven and beautifully sculpted Burton Dassett Hills are soon followed by the golden villages of Avon Dassett, Warmington and Ratley, leading to the wooded crest of Edge Hill and some contrasting scenery. Walking the length of Edge Hill with its echos of a battle long ago, you will see the Vale of the Red Horse spread out to the west. The Way crosses it in a lowland interlude through the Tysoes and Whatcote before the climb over Idlicote Hill.

Shipston on Stour is a little Georgian town reached by a short excursion from the main route. The final section includes three of the CW's loveliest villages, Honington, Tredington and Ilmington. Gasp with delight, but save breath for the final climb over a shoulder of Meon Hill, where you are on the northern tip of the Cotswolds and near the Gloucestershire border. The long trek ends at Upper Quinton, a quiet village, so you must arrange your own reception committee. But look out over the broad green; there is the welcoming Centenary Way commemorative seat.

Using the Guide

This guide gives full step by step directions for walking the Centenary Way from North to South and South to North. The route is waymarked with Warwickshire's bear and ragged staff logo, but in many places the plaques and arrows are not sufficient to show a direction, and waymarks and road signs are often damaged or disappear. For these reasons the directions are written as if they did not exist.

You will see that the directions are also quite separate from the description and comment, very terse and set in short, narrow, numbered paragraphs in a clear and open typeface. These and less obvious features have been adopted for Walkways books after much thought and experience. They aim to give information in easily located and remembered blocks of convenient size, bearing in mind that you will be reading them on the move.

Distances in *yards* or *miles* are to give you a ROUGH idea how far to walk. You do not need to measure because you will be given something to look out for, such as a stile or gate. Distances in *paces* are given to be COUNTED out if you need to. These are infrequent and only for a few yards at a time. Paces vary but you can allow for being tall or short. The reason for all this is that people carry a pace with them but not usually a measuring tape, and very few of us have got a clue what 300 yards actually looks like.

We have avoided abbreviations except for L and R, which you can probably work out. From time to time you will see "half" R or L, meaning a half turn, or about 45 degrees. Therefore "bear" R or L means a narrower angle than a half turn, or just tending away from straight ahead.

The maps are sketches to an approximate scale of 2.5ins/1mile (4cms/1km) and designed to confirm where you are rather than for route finding. The big black arrow on each map points north, but you had guessed as much, hadn't you?

Paragraphs have letters and numbers; the northbound route to Kingsbury Water Park - eg **(N33)**, and southbound to Upper Quinton - eg **(S41)**. These appear at intervals on the maps; N numbers on the right and S on the left.

You will find it helpful to carry Ordnance Survey Landranger (1.25ins/1mile) maps to help you find starting points, for general interest and in case you want to leave the route.

You should find your way very well from our directions and sketch maps, but some people like to carry the more detailed Ordnance Survey Pathfinder (2.5ins/1mile) series. We have therefore listed the relevant sheets of both series.

Amendment Service

The countryside changes all the time. You could meet new tracks, stiles and barns; hedges vanish, trees fall down and paths may be diverted. To keep directions as up to date as possible WALKWAYS issues amendment slips.

IF you write to tell me of any changes or problems you meet and tell me the paragraph number, I will refund your postage.

IF you send a stamped addressed envelope with a note of what publication(s) you have, I will send you up to date amendment slips. (Phone enquiries 0121 550 3158.)

John Roberts

Ordnance Survey Maps

Landranger Maps (1.50,000) (1.25 ins/mile) (2 cms/km)

139 Birmingham, 140 Leicester & Coventry 151 Stratford

Pathfinder Maps (1:25,000) (2.5 ins/mile) (4 cms/km)

914 SP 29/39 Nuneaton,
935 SP 28/38 Coventry (North) & Meriden
936 SP 48/58 Lutterworth,
955 SP 27/37 Coventry (South) & Kenilworth
956 SP 47/57 Rugby,
976 SP 26/36 Warwick & Royal Leamington Spa
998 SP 25/35 Stratford upon Avon (East),
999 SP 45/55 Byfield & Badby (a corner only),
1020 SP 04/14 Vale of Evesham,
1021 SP 24/34 Shipston on Stour & Edge Hill,
1022 SP 44/54 Banbury (North) (a corner only),

The Country Code

* Enjoy the countryside and respect its life and work
* Guard against all risk of fire
* Fasten all gates
* Keep your dogs under close control
* Keep to public paths across farmland
* Use gates and stiles to cross fences, hedges and walls
* Leave livestock, crops and machinery alone
* Take your litter home
* Help to keep water clean
* Protect wildlife, plants and trees
* Take special care on country roads
* Make no unnecessary noise

General Map

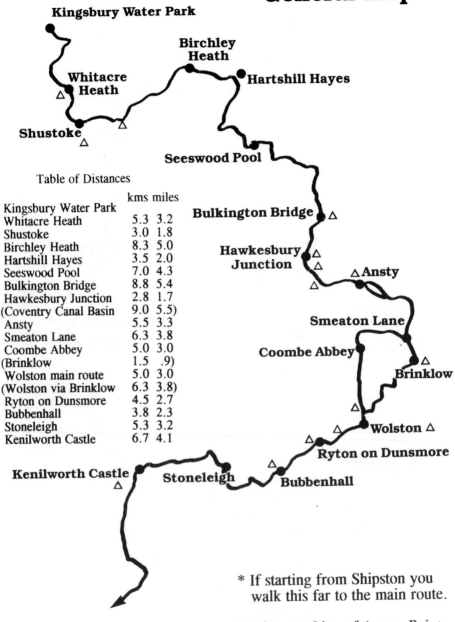

Kingsbury Water Park

Birchley Heath

Whitacre Heath

Hartshill Hayes

Shustoke

Seeswood Pool

Table of Distances

	kms	miles
Kingsbury Water Park		
Whitacre Heath	5.3	3.2
Shustoke	3.0	1.8
Birchley Heath	8.3	5.0
Hartshill Hayes	3.5	2.0
Seeswood Pool	7.0	4.3
Bulkington Bridge	8.8	5.4
Hawkesbury Junction	2.8	1.7
(Coventry Canal Basin	9.0	5.5)
Ansty	5.5	3.3
Smeaton Lane	6.3	3.8
Coombe Abbey	5.0	3.0
(Brinklow	1.5	.9)
Wolston main route	5.0	3.0
(Wolston via Brinklow	6.3	3.8)
Ryton on Dunsmore	4.5	2.7
Bubbenhall	3.8	2.3
Stoneleigh	5.3	3.2
Kenilworth Castle	6.7	4.1

Bulkington Bridge

Hawkesbury Junction

Ansty

Smeaton Lane

Coombe Abbey

Brinklow

Wolston

Ryton on Dunsmore

Kenilworth Castle

Stoneleigh

Bubbenhall

* If starting from Shipston you walk this far to the main route.

△ Pubs, see *List of Access Points* for details.

(8)

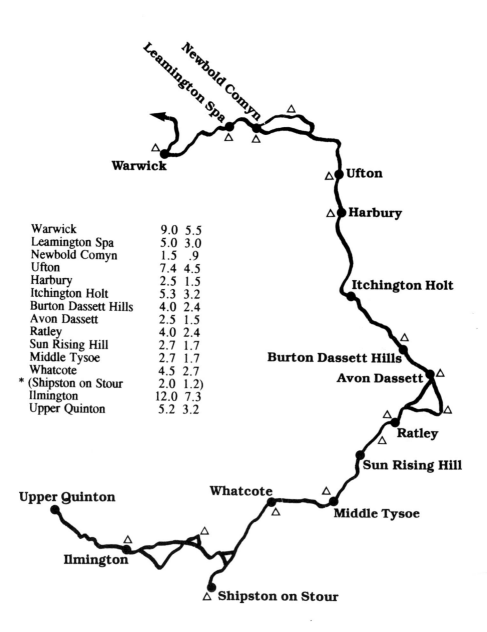

Warwick

Leamington Spa

Newbold Comyn

Ufton

Harbury

Itchington Holt

Burton Dassett Hills

Avon Dassett

Ratley

Sun Rising Hill

Middle Tysoe

Whatcote

Upper Quinton

Ilmington

Shipston on Stour

Warwick	9.0	5.5
Leamington Spa	5.0	3.0
Newbold Comyn	1.5	.9
Ufton	7.4	4.5
Harbury	2.5	1.5
Itchington Holt	5.3	3.2
Burton Dassett Hills	4.0	2.4
Avon Dassett	2.5	1.5
Ratley	4.0	2.4
Sun Rising Hill	2.7	1.7
Middle Tysoe	2.7	1.7
Whatcote	4.5	2.7
* (Shipston on Stour	2.0	1.2)
Ilmington	12.0	7.3
Upper Quinton	5.2	3.2

List of Access Points & Pubs

Here we list useful places for starting or finishing Centenary Way walks, and their names appear in the book as bold headings. We have also listed pubs in between. Directions start afresh from each place (but not from pubs), so walkers already en route may find the wording a bit odd or superfluous, but still clear. Of course, you can join the route at any other point, but will have to find the correct paragraph.

We note the precise point at which the CW arrives at each place, eg "Boot & Blister Inn", and this is mentioned in the directions. Most Access Points have spaces for parking cars and public transport connections, but wherever you start, please do not park where it might cause inconvenience. Never use pub car parks without permission.

Kingsbury Water Park (SP 204960) (S1) Visitor Centre on west side of lakes .8 mile west of Kingsbury. WCs, cafe, pay (a lot) car park - check closing time. Buses and free car park at Kingsbury village .8 mile away. To walk between them see *Transport & Accommodation.*

Whitacre Heath (SP 219928) (S8) (N202) Swan Inn at T junction on B4114 2 miles south of Kingsbury. General store, Railway Inn, phone, roadside parking, buses.

Shustoke (SP 228909) (S14) (N196) Plough Inn on B4114 south of reservoir. Phone, roadside parking.

(Pub) Bull's Head, Furnace End on B4114 east of Shustoke Reservoirs.

Birchley Heath (SP 286946) (S28) (N182) Bus shelter on green in hamlet at south tip of Bentley Park Wood. Phone, roadside parking, buses.

Hartshill Hayes (SP 317944) (S34d) Visitor Centre in Country Park 3.5 miles north-west of Nuneaton. WCs, refreshments Sat, Sun & Bank Holidays. Pay car park (check closing time). Bus - Hartshill 1 mile.

Seeswood Pool (SP 330904) (S52) (N160) on B4102 2.5 miles south-west of Nuneaton. Park on wide verges a few hundred yards west. Buses on B4112.

Bulkington Bridge (SP 372868) (S61) (N149) Canal bridge on B4029 over Coventry Canal. Navigation Inn. Park in side road, bus. Bedworth Station .5 mile west.

Hawkesbury Junction (SP 362846) (S61X) (N147X) Canal junction just north of B4109 Bulkington - Coventry road. Greyhound Inn, free parking .25 mile at Grange Road on Coventry Arm, buses on B4113 .3 mile west.

Coventry Canal Basin (SP 333795) Canal terminus and warehouses etc at Draper's Field on north side of City Ring Road by A444 Nuneaton road. You have a 5.5 mile towpath walk to to join the Way at Hawkesbury Junction.

(Pub) Elephant & Castle on Oxford Canal at Trusses Bridge on on B4109.

(Pub) Jolly Colliers, at Sowe Common by Oxford Canal, on south side of M6.

Ansty (SP 398833) (S63) (N147) Canal bridge in village on B4065 1 mile north of M6/M69 junction. Rose & Castle, phone, park carefully in side road by canal. Buses.

Smeaton Lane (SP 428807) (S70a) or (S71) (N140) T junction .5 mile south of Coombe Fields Farm. Verge parking.

Coombe Abbey (SP 403796) (S76) (N135) Visitor Centre at Country Park on B4027 Coventry - Lutterworth road. WC, restaurant/coffee shop, telephone, pay car park (and how) - check closing time, buses.

Brinklow (SP 436795) (S70d) (N131i) *[on alternative route]* Raven Inn in village on B4027 Coventry - Lutterworth road. Shop, pubs, roadside parking, buses.

(Pub) Royal Oak in Brandon.

Wolston (SP 412756) (S81) (N130) War Memorial in village 2 miles north-west of A45 at Ryton on Dunsmore. Pubs, fish bar, shops, phones, roadside parking, bus.

(Cafe) Ryton Gardens at National Centre For Organic Gardening. Leave Way as noted on map after paras (S85) or (N124).

Ryton on Dunsmore (SP 386743) (S90) (N122) Blacksmith's Arms in High Street on south west side of A45. Shops, balti takeaway, telephone, roadside parking, bus.

Bubbenhall (SP 362725) (S97) (N116) Malt Shovel in village on A445 - Leamington Spa to Ryton on Dunsmore. Three Horse Shoes, phone, roadside parking, bus.

Stoneleigh (SP 330726) (S106X) (N106X) Church in village 2 miles east of Kenilworth. Telephone, park in rough layby on east side of road bridge, bus.

Kenilworth Castle (SP 280724) (S118) (N96) Queen & Castle Inn by B4103 west of town. All facilities near, WCs in Abbey Fields. Free castle car park, buses.

Warwick (SP 282650) (S129) (N84) St Mary's church. All facilities, pay car park in Theatre St, free parking at Racecourse (600yds), buses, trains.

Leamington Spa (SP 318655) (S135) (N77) Royal Pump Rooms on The Parade. All facilities, buses, trains.

Newbold Comyn (SP 329659) (S137) (N75) Leisure Centre in Country Park on east side of Leamington. Newbold Comyn Arms, cafe, WCs, free parking.

(Pub) Stag's Head at Offchurch.

Ufton (SP 379621) (S142) (N69) White Hart Inn in village on A425 Leamington Spa - Southam road. Cottage Tea Room & Restaurant on A425, Post Office, phone, roadside parking in lane by inn, buses.

Harbury (SP 374598) (S147) (N63) Village Hall in village 4.5 miles south-east of Leamington Spa. Pubs, shops, phone, roadside parking, buses.

Itchington Holt (SP 373553) (S153) (N57) Rough layby on B4451 400yds north of Junction 12 of M40. No facilites.

(Pub) Red Lion in Northend.

Burton Dassett Hills (SP 395521) (S157) (N52) Stone beacon in Country Park 2.5 miles south-east of Gaydon (near Junction 12 of M40). Pay (lots) car park, WCs.

Avon Dassett (SP 410500) (S161) (N48) Prince Rupert in village 1.4 miles south-east of above. Phone, roadside parking, buses.

(Pub) The Plough at Warmington.

Ratley (SP 381475) (S167) (N44) Junction at top of village .5 mile south-west of B4086 Banbury - Stratford road. Rose & Crown, free car park on Town Hill 150yds south of CW, phone, buses.

(Pub) Castle Inn at Edge Hill.

Sun Rising Hill (SP 363458) (S171X) (N38X) Track meets road at top of hill on A422 Banbury - Stratford road. Layby parking just east of CW, phone.

Middle Tysoe (SP 341443) (S176a)/(S177) (N35) Peacock Inn in village 5.5 miles north-east of Shipston on Stour Shops, phone, roadside parking, buses.

Whatcote (SP 300446) (S184) (N27) Royal Oak in hamlet 3.75 miles north-east of Shipston on Stour. Phone, roadside parking.

Shipston on Stour (SP 259406) (S189e) (N18c) on A3400 Stratford - Oxford road. Free car park in Telegraph Street, all facilities, buses.

(Pub) White Lion at Tredington.

Ilmington (SP 213437) (S198) (N12) Howard Arms in village 3.5 mile north-west of Shipston on Stour. Red Lion, shop, phone, roadside parking, buses.

Upper Quinton (SP 177465) (N1) Commemorative CW seat on Green in village 5.5 miles south of Stratford upon Avon. College Arms, Gay Dog, and buses are .75 mile away in Lower Quinton. To walk between the two see *Transport & Accommodation* section - FEET.

St John the Baptist, Avon Dassett

(14)

Linked Long Distance Paths

The Centenary Way meets these other trails and we note below the nearest Access Points.

Heart of England Way - Kingsbury Water Park and Upper Quinton.

Sowe Valley Path - Hawkesbury Junction

Midland Link - (planned by Walkways) between Kenilworth and Baddesley Clinton on the Heart of England Way, and west to the Forehill Picnic Site to meet the North Worcestershire Path. This leads to the Staffordshire Way and Worcestershire Way.

Grand Union Canal Walk - Warwick and Newbold Comyn.

Macmillan Way - Avon Dassett, Warmington, Ratley and Sun Rising Hill

Monarch's Way - Upper Quinton

Warwickshire County Council also plans a Millenium Way in the Forest of Arden. Details to be announced.

Transport & Accommodation

ACCOMMODATION
For a free print out of bed & breakfast places at convenient intervals all along the Way, send a stamped, addressed envelope to "Centenary List", 8 Hillside Close, Bartley Green, Birmingham B32 4LT.

Tourist Information Offices also have addresses and the following are all on or near the Centenary Way.

Tamworth - Town Hall, Market Street - 01827 59134
Nuneaton - The Library, Church Street - 01203 384027.
Coventry - Bayley Lane - 01203 832303.
Kenilworth - The Library, Smalley Place - 01926 52595.
Warwick - The Court House, Jury Street - 01926 492212.
Leamington Spa - The Lodge, Jephson Gardens - 01926
311470

RAIL
There are railway stations at Bedworth, Warwick and Leamington Spa which are on or close to the Way.

From Coventry station you can walk across the City and follow the Coventry Canal. (See *Access Points etc.*)

The following stations are more distant but might be useful; Birmingham New Street, Water Orton, Tamworth, Two Gates, Atherstone, Nuneaton, Stratford upon Avon, Banbury, Moreton in Marsh.

All rail enquiries can be made on 0121 643 2711.

BUSES
Many bus services, frequent and otherwise, connect with the Centenary Way, and obviously the Access Points we have listed are not exclusive. Since services may be altered or stopped we can only mention the Access Points at which there were services when this was written, and refer you to Warwickshire County Council's Busline on 01926 414140

CAR
You can motor to any of the Access Points, but at some of them parking space is very limited. If you want to leave more than one car we suggest you check in advance.

FEET
These directions enable you to join or leave the Centenary Way
on foot at certain points:

Kingsbury Water Park (.8 mile)

Kingsbury Village to Visitor Centre

(1) Go to bus shelter behind White Swan. Take track (then path) to church. Pass it on your L & take steps down to cross River Tame.

(2) Follow causeway & cross bridge. Take track ahead with pools on your L to posts 12 & 13.

(3) Go L over bridge & fork R to Visitor Centre.

Visitor Centre to Kingsbury Village

(a) From Visitor Centre door, go L past other buildings & join tarmac path to drive. Take path opposite (under power lines), forking L to cross bridge & join track.

(b) Go R with lakes on your R 450yds (ignore L fork) & cross bridge.

(c) Follow causeway, cross River Tame & follow path & steps to pass church. Take track to road & bus shelter R.

Wintry lakeshore at Kingsbury Water Park

Boots & Clothes & Things

If you are an experienced walker you can skip this bit. If you are not, there are many books and frequent magazine articles offering expert advice on what to wear. In addition you may like to consider these basic points.

(1) **Boots**. Most people seem to prefer them at most times of year. Think about the extra energy you need to swing, say, 200 grams more than you need some 1,200 times per mile, and don't buy ones that feel heavy. Trainers are excellent in dry weather but consider replacing the footbeds with a shock absorbing type.

(2) **Socks**. You don't necessarily need two pairs, but a good thickness of woolly padding is a great comfort. The traditional grey rough wool "rag sock" is hardwearing and fairly thick, but that is about all. Try loop pile socks.

(3) **Gaiters** can prevent rain creeping down your legs and into your socks and boots. They also work for quick stream crossings and keep you comfortable through mud and undergrowth.

(4) **Jeans** are cut too close for comfortable walking. Denim is hot in summer, cold in winter and holds the damp. In summer try polycotton trousers, which are light and dry in no time. In colder weather corduroy is not bad.

(5) Take a **waterproof,** preferably hooded and long enough to reach down to your gaiters.

(6) Take a **hat, gloves** and something to **keep out the wind** such as a showerproof jacket. Your waterproof would do, but they can be sweaty. Always carry an extra sweater.

Upper Quinton (.5 mile)

*Upper Quinton
to Lower Quinton*

*Lower Quinton
to Upper Quinton*

(1)   Follow   road   to non-tower end of church and take small gate into churchyard.   Go ahead & cross stile. Bear R to field corner power poles to cross stile & culvert.

(2) Go R on fenced track & cross stile L. Follow R hedge, round field corner plus 50yds, & cross stiles R.

(3) Go L by hedge till   it bends R, then cross R to projecting hedge end. Go L by hedge & cross corner stile to track. Go R to gate/stile and lane. Go   L to "The Green".

(a) From T junction by sign "The Green", go R past last house R (& its drive) & cross stile by double   gates.   Follow track past end of hedge L & cross stile L.

(b) Follow L hedge to its end & cross field R to hedge.   Go L by hedge to cross stiles R. Go L & follow hedge round field corner   to next corner, & cross stile.

(c) Go R on fenced track to   cross   culvert   L   & stile. Bear L & cross midhedge   stile   to churchyard. Go ahead to small gate & road. Go L to bus stops, etc, etc.

No room on the Centenary Way seat, Upper Quinton

(7) Consider long sleeved, **brushed cotton shirts** which open all down the front. You can wear them open or buttoned to various degrees (or not at all), with sleeves rolled up or down, inside or outside your trousers, and have ventilation or protection from sun, wind, vegetation and insects.

(8) Lastly, something hardly ever mentioned - **water**. Experiments suggest that people who drink it liberally can walk much further and feel far less tired than those who do not. A litre is not too much too carry. Don't buy a fancy water bottle, a pop bottle will do.

This is general advice based mainly on ordinary clothing. Visit a good outdoor equipment shop and see if they have anything to offer which would improve your comfort. There are windproof polyester fleeces and magic vests which do not stay wet like cotton shirts. First though, try ordinary clothes to find out whether and how they can be improved upon.

".... take an extra sweater." Arlescote

Warwickshire's
Centenary Way

Main Map Symbols

Access Point	●
Path	· · · · · · · · ·
Track	- - - - - ‿ ⌐
Road/lane	≺
Railway	＋＋＋＋＋＋
Canal	⊥ ⊥ ⊥ ⊥
Stream/river/lake	～～◯～
Woodland	⌣⌣⌣
Hedge/fence	⊤
Church	+
Building	▴
Pub	△

Maps are drawn to an approximate
scale of 2.5ins/1 mile - 4cms/1km.

(21)

(S1) From door of Visitor Centre go L. Pass other buildings & follow tarmac footpath to drive. Take path opposite to lake.

(S2) Go R by lake & pass sailing club to drive. Take path opposite, follow to cross footbridge & bear L to drive.

(S3) Go R & round L bend, plus 25 paces. Take track R to lake corner, then L to next corner & step R onto drive.

(S4) Cross drive to behind car barrier. Head for conifers & bear L on causeway path. Cross foot-bridge, meet path from L & rejoin drive. Follow drive appx 300yds to bollards before steel bridge.
[Hemlingford Bridge]

(S5) DON'T CROSS. Go R by river & under A4097, plus 25yds. Go R on grass track .8 mile to road.

(S6) Cross into entrance opposite & take track on its R. Follow .8 mile to road. [Lea Marston]

(N203) Take path R by 30mph sign & follow .8 mile to road.

(N204) Take track opposite .8 mile to River Tame ahead. Go L under A4097 to bridge. DON'T CROSS.
(Hemlingford Bridge)

(N205) Go L on drive to 1st R bend. Go round it plus a few paces & bear L to lakeside path. At fork go L on causeway path (via bridge) & bear R to rejoin drive.

(N206) Cross to pool. Take path L beside it to corner, then go R to drive. Go L & round R bend plus a few paces to take path L.

(N207) Follow to cross footbridge & on to corner of drive. Take path opposite past sailing club R to far corner of lake. Go L to Visitor Centre at

Kingsbury Water Park

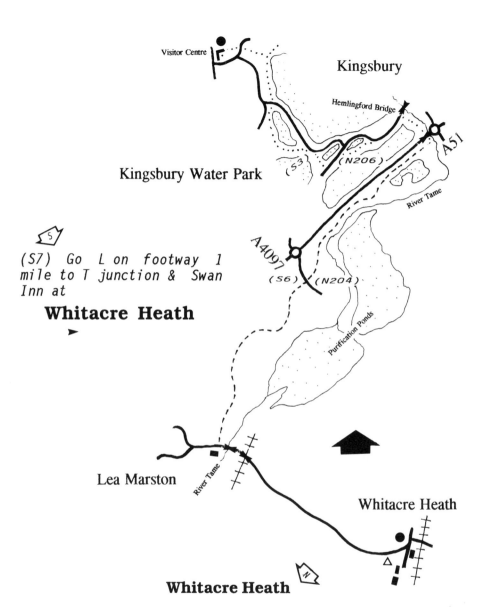

Visitor Centre

Kingsbury

Hemlingford Bridge

Kingsbury Water Park

(S3) (N206)

A51

River Tame

(S7) *Go L on footway 1 mile to T junction & Swan Inn at*

A4097

(S6) (N204)

Whitacre Heath

Purification Ponds

Lea Marston

River Tame

Whitacre Heath

Whitacre Heath

(N202) *Take footway of road opposite pub 1 mile. Cross railway & river to red house L. [Lea Marston]*

Whitacre Heath

(S8) Face pub, go L & take 1st road R. Cross bridge to base of slope. Turn sharp R on track & follow by railway .3 mile to gate

(S9) Go L with hedge & cross plank bridge, then to far L field corner & cross twin stiles.

(S10) Go R by hedge (via plank bridge) & on 200yds to cross plank bridge R. Go L by hedge & take corner gap, then with railway on your R to bridge & lane.

(S11) Go L 50yds to entrance R & cross stile. Follow R hedge 150yds & cross stile R. Go L on enclosed path to stile & railway.

(S12) GREAT CARE. Cross & take stile. Go R on field edge, round corner & on to near power pole.

(S13) Bear L on crossfield path (via bridge & stile) to B4114. Go L to Plough Inn at

Shustoke

(N195) Go R by hedge to join lane, & follow .4 mile to B4114 at

Shustoke

(N196) Face Plough Inn, go R .25 mile to entrance R, & take tarmac fieldpath.

(N197) Follow via stile & bridge & on to next hedge. Go R, round field corner & cross stile L to railway.

(N198) GREAT CARE. Cross line & take stile. Follow enclosed path 200yds & cross stile R. Go L by hedge to stile & lane.

(N199) Go L 30yds & cross stile R before bridge. Follow L hedge to field corner & take gap ahead. Go with hedge on your R to near spinney & cross plank R.

(N200) Go L with hedge (via plank) to field corner & cross twin stiles L. Go parallel with R hedge to cross plank. Follow R hedge to gate/stile & track.

(N201) Follow railside track .3 mile (via R bend) to road. Go L to junction & L to Swan Inn at

Whitacre Heath

Heart of England Way

(N201)

(S10)

(S12)
(N198)

Shustoke Reservoirs

B4114

Shustoke

(S15)

(N193)

Furnace End

B4114

(N192) Go L 350yds & take gate/stile R. Go L by bank (via gate/stile) to field corner.

(N193) Go L under railway & cross stile. Go R & cross corner stile. Follow R fence to end & cross stile.

(N194) Follow path 50yds & take gate/stile L. Follow grass track to turning circle. Join track past reservoir, cross bridge, round L bend to house & cross stile ahead.

(S14) Opposite pub, take Bixhill Lane .4 mile. Where lane kinks L thro gateway, take wide hedge gap ahead. Go with hedge on your L to pass house & cross stile L.

(S15) Follow tarmac drive, round R bend & pass lake to turning circle. Continue on grass past plastic gizmos L to gate, & cross stile. ▾

(S16) Go R & cross stile. Go L by fence & cross field corner stile. Follow L hedge to cross stile L & pass under railway.

(S17) Go R by bank via gate/stile to next field corner & take gate/stile to B4114. Go L to crossroads. [Furnace End] ▸

(25)

Kingsbury Water Park is the legacy of fifty years of gravel extraction which left a chain of water-filled pits in the Tame Valley. From 1973 Warwickshire County Council transformed some of them into scenic lakes, and now these Warwickshire broads are full of interest and aquatic beauty. The 600-acre park includes more than thirty lakes fringed with reeds, mosses, brambles, birch, willows, alders and oak, which support a rich variety of birds and insects.

Kingsbury's great church, with its Norman doorway, 14th century tower and 16th century belfry, overlooks the spreading lakes. Next door stands the stone Elizabethan hall, now a farm, on a site where the Saxon kings of Mercia are said to have built a palace. Nearby stands Kingsbury Mill, successor to a mill rated for tax in the Domesday Book in 1086 at 9s 3d, or 46p. The 18th century building produced gun-barrels for use against Napoleon, then became in turn a saw mill, paper mill, leather mill, electrified grain mill and other things, leaving it rather the worse for wear.

The CW runs by the River Tame and past more great pools, then over an horizon-broadening hillock and by purification lakes to Lea Marston. These still and odorous waters are unique in Britain. The Tame is the most polluted river in the Severn Trent region, graded as E on the NRA's A - F scale. The pools slow down its flow, allowing the worst pollutants to settle so that it continues approaching Grade D, and supporting some coarse fish. The road to Whitacre Heath passes a Warwickshire Wildlife Trust reserve and Site of Special Scientific Interest (access for Trust members only). Snipe, redshank and hunting owls occupy old gravel pits, reed beds and rough grassland.

When crossing the railway line before Shustoke, look west to the Venetian Gothic gables and roofs of Nether Whitacre Pumping Station (1885). One of its two James Watt beam engines is in the Birmingham Science Museum. Shustoke's Plough Inn stands by an old animal pound amongst a few cottages. Down a lane by the inn is a village green, backed

by an immense former farmhouse, gabled and timber-framed.
The nearby reservoirs of strangely contrasting size, 90.5 and
8.5 acres, supply water to Coventry and Nuneaton. They make
a pleasant walk but suffer from algal growth, probably due to
surlpus nitrate fertilizers, which is partly controlled by
bales of straw.

There are no furnaces today - no industry at all - at Furnace
End, just a pub, a butcher's shop, a few handsome old houses
and some modern ones (less handsome). But during the 17th
century the Jennens family, Birmingham ironmasters, bought
Whitacre Hall and built furnaces here. The most famous of
the Jennens was Charles, born in 1700 and known from his
lavish life-style at the palatial Gopsall Hall as Soliman the
Magnificent. He became a staunch patron of Handel and
contributed the libretto of *The Messiah*.

Hoar Park Wood is a remnant of the ancient Forest of Arden.
Just inside are traces of an old pack-horse trail which once
linked Birmingham and Atherstone. You meet it again near
the former coal mining village of Birchley Heath.

Kingsbury Water Park

(27)

(S18) Go R (B4114) 280yds (past last house L to road sign) & cross stile L.

(S19) Follow R hedge via 2 fields to stile & lane. Go L .3 mile to concrete drive R by road junction.

(S20) Take concrete drive past house to R bend & cross stile L. Follow L hedge via 3 stiles & cross plank bridge to field.

(S21) Follow L hedge 30 paces to corner. Cross midfield past circular concrete water tank to take corner gate.

(S22) Follow L hedge & cross corner stile. Go on by R hedge 50yds & cross stile R. Go L by hedge (past Hoar Park Wood & via corner gap) to cross footbridge.

(S23) Go ahead across field corner & continue with brook on your R (via 2 stiles) to enter copse.

(S24) Exit by stile. Follow R field edge by brook .3 mile, & take wide gateway to track. ▶

(N185) Follow L edge of field (by brook) .3 mile to TALL trees, & cross stile L.

(N186) Go thro spinney & cross stile. Continue by brook (via stile) & cross footbridge.

(N187) Follow R hedge past Hoar Park Wood plus 50yds & cross stile R. Go L & cross stile, then follow R hedge to field corner.

(N188) Take L of 2 gateways. DON'T FOLLOW COW TRACK, bear L past circular concrete water tank to projecting hedge corner.

(N189) Go with hedge on your R 25 yds to field corner & cross stile, plank & stile. Follow R hedge (via stiles) to join concrete track.

(N190) Follow to lane, (junction with B4116 is R). Go L on lane .3 mile (past 1st gate R & 2nd) to cross stile R.

(N191) Follow L hedge (via 2 fields) to B4114. Go R to crossroads. [Furnace End] ◀

(28)

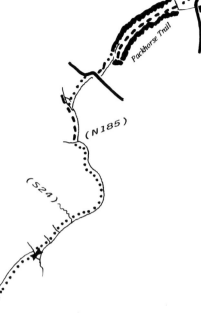

(S25) Follow 200yds (via gate) & cross stile R. Cross plank & 2 stiles, then follow R field edge to stile & lane.

(S26) Go R to bend. Take 1st gateway L & climb ramp to field. Go ahead 30yds to take steps & stile R.

(S27) Go L & follow wooded track [Packhorse Trail] .4 mile to stile & green. Walk its length to road at

Birchley Heath
►

Birchley Heath

(N182) From bus shelter, walk full length of green & cross stile. Follow wooded track (Packhorse Trail) .4 mile to end, & cross stile R.

(N183) Climb steps & go L 30yds to gate & lane. Go R to R bend & climb bank L to cross hidden stile.

(N184) Go L down hedge to cross stiles & plank - to track. Go L 200yds via gate/stile & enter wide gateway.
◄

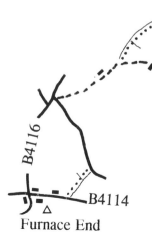

Birchley Heath

(S28) Put green on your L & go 200yds to last house R. Take road R to end.

(S29) Go ahead by R hedge to field corner, then L to next corner & cross stile. Cut R across corner to cross plank & stile.

(S30) Go with hedge on your R to approach farm. Bear L round concrete tank & cross stile to track.

(S31) Go L past sheds to track junction & cross stile ahead. Follow L hedge to cross stile L. Go ahead to stile & road.

(S32) Go L & take lane R. Follow .3 mile to L bend at Oldbury Picnic Area.

(S33) Enter Area, go L to end & cross 2 stiles. Follow cutting 230yds & cross stile. Go on 30yds & cross stile L.

(S34) Follow R hedge (via 2 stiles) to hedge corner, & keep same line to projecting hedge corner. Go with hedge on your L round field corner plus 200yds, to stile L by projecting fence. see note on EXCURSION

(N176) Put your back to stile & go R. Round field corner to next hedge corner. Go ahead to projecting hedge corner.

(N177) Go with hedge on your L via 3 stiles to old railway. Go R via 3 stiles & up grass area to Oldbury Cutting Picnic Area.

(N178) Exit to lane & go L .3 mile to T junction. Go L 100yds & cross stile R.

(N179) Go ahead & cross stile. Go R by hedge to stile & track junction. (Lady Wood Farm) Go ahead past sheds & cross stile R

(N180) Go L past corner of concrete tank to join L hedge. Follow to field corner & cross stile & plank. Cut L across field corner & take stile.

(N181) Follow L hedge to field corner, then R to reach service road & main road. Go L 200yds to green at

Birchley Heath
◄

►

(30)

Birchley Heath

Lady Wood Farm

****
EXCURSION
The Way continues along this hedge but includes a "there & back" excursion to Hartshill Hayes Country Park.
****

Hartshill Hayes

Moor Wood Farm

Oldbury Cutting
Picnic Area

(S34a) Cross stile & go ahead over field corner to cross stile, then gate/ stile R onto track.

(S34b) Follow to quarry, then ahead on fenced track to corner by gates. Go R on fenced path to end & cross stile.

(S34c) Head 25yds R of red roof & on to field corner stile & lane. Follow drive opposite to corner & take gate. Bear R round fenced reservoir to Visitor Centre at

Hartshill Hayes

(S34d) Put buildings on your R & head for fenced reservoir. Bear R & walk round it then take gate to drive. ◄

(S34e) Follow to lane & ◄cross stile opposite. Pass double power pole with gizmo on your L, cross crest & go down to stile & fenced path.

(S34f) Follow to gates, then L to quarry. Bear R & down to take gate/stile. Cross stile L & go ahead to stile & field.

NEXT paras
Southbound - (S35) ►
◄*Northbound - (N176)*
****

(31)

From Birchley Heath fieldpaths and a lane lead the Centenary Way to Oldbury Cutting Picnic Area. This was part of a mine railway line which we meet again at Ansley Common; there are fine views south. Following fieldpaths towards Hartshill Hayes, you pass the back of Moorwood Rare Breed Leisure Farm. It is one of several centres for preserving breeds of sheep, cattle, pigs and poultry no longer used by farmers, such as the Tamworth and Gloucester Old Spot pigs.

The top of the immense hill of Hartshill Hayes is a 136 acre Country Park. It is mostly woodland, a small remnant of the ancient Forest of Arden, though largely replanted in the late 18th century. From the crest at 560 feet the ground shelves steeply to the Anker Valley and Coventry Canal. From the ridge visitors can gaze across Leicestershire to the rocky tors of Charnwood Forest and, perhaps, the heights of the Peak District. Arthur Mee wrote in his *Warwickshire* that on the plain you could count forty churches. Look out for the ghost, a young girl who runs downhill on calm spring days with hair and cloak billowing in a ghostly wind.

The Midlands lies mainly upon geologically recent rocks laid down under successive seas, deserts and forests. But in this area is one of only four small outcrops of ancient volcanic rock in the region. Geology, scenery, history and literature mingle here. Oldbury Camp was an Iron Age hillfort. The grassy mound, on the other hand, is a reservoir built circa 1977 to hold 15 million gallons of water. The Romans came in AD60, finished off Queen Boudicca in the Anker valley and settled down to make glass and pottery in kilns whose remains have been found nearby. Their descendants at Atherstone turned to hatting and used lime wood from these woodlands for the blocks upon which the headgear was moulded. In 1125 Hugh de Hardreshull built a castle of which bits survive near Hartshill village, and here the poet Michael Drayton, Shakespeare's contemporary, was born.

Within a mile of the Hayes you reach Common Farm and pass under the same old railway as at Oldbury Cutting

to reach Ansley Common. The small building in a field
north-east of Common Farm is an old pump-house covering
a 90ft shaft. Built about 1880 by the local mine-owner, it
rupplied the village with pure, clear water which the farmer
still draws. Ansley Common is just a linear mining village
of cheap, sturdy houses. But like many mining settlements,
the setting is very pleasant and the village makes the best
of itself by lining the street with lime trees. The local
mine closed in the 1960s, as have so many others in this
coalfield. But their legacy lives on in small, isolated
villages and strange green mountains that seem at odds
with the local geography.

From high ground near Bret's Hall Wood, you can see another
industrial monument, the pointed, granite spoil heap known as
the Warwickshire Matterhorn or Mount Judd, at Judd's Quarry,
Nuneaton. We cross another man made hill at Galley Common,
the spoil heap of Haunchwood Colliery (closed 1967). When it
was reclaimed by the county council in 1974, 25 metres were
lopped of the summit by shifting 750,000 cubic metres of
spoil. Its height was halved and the sides made less steep,
so sheep now graze the bare, green hilltop which lolls in a
landscape of small fields and mature hedgerows like a
benevolent whale.

Footbridge near Galley Common

(33)

(S35) From stile by projecting fence, pass end of fence & follow field edge. Round corner to next corner & cross stiles & plank L.

(S36) Go half R (ignore metal stile L) to cross wooden one. Go ahead via gate to track. [Common Farm] Follow round R bend & across estate road to B4114. [Ansley Common]

(S37) Cross & go R 170yds to Limes Coppice. Take fenced tarmac path L to cross stile.

(S38) Go half L to 10yds past hedge corner trees & cross stile. Follow R hedge to its corner, then go ahead & cross stile. Skirt wood [Bret's Hall Wood] on your R & cross corner stile.

(S39) Go ahead a few paces to wood corner. Go down towards sheds via midfence stile & cross next stile to track.

(S40) Follow 200yds (past 1st stile at start of R hedge) to cross 2nd stile. Sight distant white house with mast on its L. Go ahead towards mast & cross midhedge stile.◄

(S41) Head for bottom L field corner & take gate/stile L. Go ahead (past stile R) to stile & track.

(S42) Cross stile opposite & follow L hedge to cross footbridge. Follow R hedge to field end & cross stile. Go L to road. [Galley Common] ►

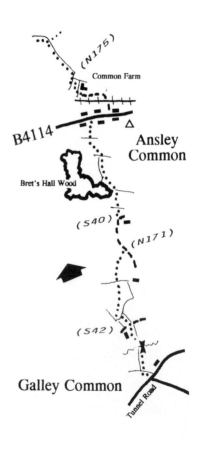

(N168) Go L to T junction. *[Galley Common]* Take gate or stile on L of gate opposite, & follow R hedge to cross stile R. Go L past shed & follow L hedge to cross footbridge.

(N169) Go ahead & follow winding R hedge to stile & track. Cross stile opposite. Bear a little L & take fieldend gate/stile.

(N170) Turn half right, go up to midhedge gap & cross stile. **AHEAD, SIGHT DISTANT HILLTOP FARM,** & head 10yds R of it to stile & track.

(N171) Go L to track end & cross stile. Bear a little L & cross stile in recessed fence corner. Go up to top corner of wood & cross stile. ◀

(N172) Go L by wood & ◀cross stile. *[Brets Hall Wood]* Go ahead to projecting hedge corner, then with hedge on your L to cross corner stile. Go half L (pass power pole on your L) to stile & path.

(N173) Follow to B4114. *[Ansley Common]* Go R 170 yds to house 126 & go L. Cross estate road & follow track to farm. *[Common Farm]*

(N174) Pass farm house on your R & take gate/stile opposite corner of black barn. Go ahead & cross stile. Go R to recessed fence corner & cross stile, plank & stile.

(N175) Go R by hedge & round field corner, plus 400yds to projecting fence with stile R.

see note re
EXCURSION - p(31)
◀

*At Bret's Hall Wood,
Ansley Common*

(S43) Take road opposite 140yds & cross stile R. Climb to mark post on summit. **NB Railway meets wood.** Head for this point & cross fence corner stile. Cross next stile to railside path.

(S44) Go R to stile & field. Curve L over tunnel mouth & cross stile. Follow path above pond to gateway & field.

(S45) Face along railway but GO HALF R. When in view, head for middle of long hedge ahead & cross stile.

(S46) Follow R hedge via 5 stiles to lane.◢

(S47) Go R 140yds to 1st flats & cross stile opposite (R). Follow R hedge to take corner gap. Go L (via gate/stile) & follow L hedge to stile & B4112. (Robinson's End)

(S48) Go L 150yds & turn R into fenced path. Follow to stile & field.

(S49) Follow R hedge 100 yds to double power pole. Cross L towards midhedge trees & take gate/stile. Follow L hedge 160yds & go R down to gate in bottom hedge.

(S50) Follow grass track & take gate/stile. Go up parallel with L hedge to cross stile, plank & stile. Follow R hedge to corner stile & B4102.

(S51) Go L .3 mile to

Seeswood Pool

▶

Galley Common

(36)

Seeswood Pool

(N160) Put pool on your R, follow road .3 mile to gate L, & cross stile just beyond.

(N161) Follow L hedge to cross stile & plank. Go parallel with R hedge & cross midhedge stile. Keep same line to gate/stile & track. Follow to next gate

(N162) Go ahead midfield to top hedge. Go L to corner gate/stile. Cross midfield to 100yds L of far R field corner. Go R by hedge & fenced path to B4112. [Robinson's End]

◀

(N163) Cross, go L 150yds to end of fence & take gate/stile R. Follow R hedge (via gate/stile) & take gap R. Follow L hedge to stile & lane.

(N164) Go L 140yds past 2nd lampost & cross stile L. Follow L hedge via 5 stiles & cross field corner stile.

(N165) **NB HOUSES AHEAD/R.** Head for BIGGEST tree on their R & take gateway.

(N166) Follow path above pond & cross stile. Curve R over tunnel mouth to stile & fenced path. Follow 200yds & cross stile L.

(N167) Cross stile ahead & go up diagonally R to summit markpost. Head for nearest red brick house & cross stile to road.

◀

Winter sunset over
Seeswood Pool

(37)

Seeswood Pool

(S52) Put pool on your L & follow footway 300yds to two gates R. Take gap or stile by L one.

(S53) Follow R hedge & cross plank to trees. Take path (fork R) & cross wooded drive to field.

(S54) Go ahead & join fenced path to track. Go R to farm.

(S55) Go R by hedge 150yds to cross stile & plank L. Go R & cross field corner stile.

(S56) Bear L across field to oak & follow bank 275 yds to markpost near gap R. Cross L to trees & go R on field edge to track.

(S57) Go L .75 mile to junction at road bend. [Bermuda Village]

(S58) Pass end of village street & take track by privet hedge. Cross A444 bridge to estate road & follow .3 mile to steel railway bridge L.

(N152) Go R .3 mile. Curve L, cross A444 bridge & follow tarmac path to road bend. [Bermuda Village]

(N153) Go ahead past street & take rising track L. Follow .75 mile past house R & thro trees.

(N154) Go R by trees, pass electrical gizmo, round next corner & on 20 paces.

(N155) Cross field L to bank & go R beside it 275 yds to oak tree.

(N156) Bear R & cross stile. Bear L up field 100yds to handrails L & cross stile. Go R by hedge to track by farm.

(N157) Go L & round R bend to end of tarmac road.

(N158) Take fenced path L, cross field & enter trees.

(N159) Cross drive & exit to field. Follow L hedge to gate & B4102. Go L to

◄ **Seeswood Pool**

(38)

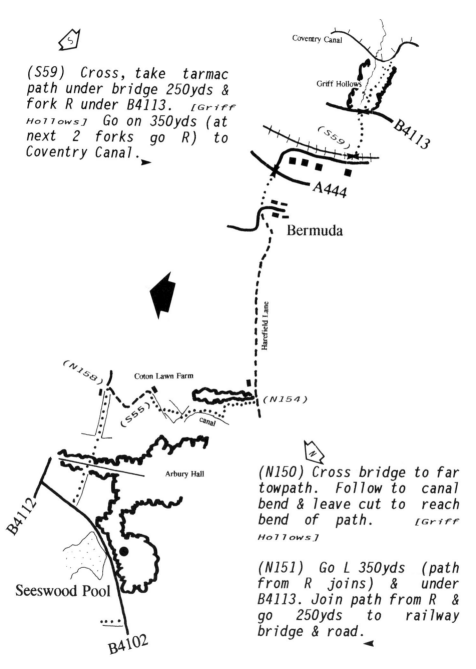

(S59) Cross, take tarmac path under bridge 250yds & fork R under B4113. [Griff Hollows] Go on 350yds (at next 2 forks go R) to Coventry Canal.

Coventry Canal

Griff Hollows

(S59)

B4113

A444

Bermuda

Harefield Lane

(N158)

Coton Lawn Farm

(S55)

canal

(N154)

Arbury Hall

B4112

Seeswood Pool

B4102

(N150) Cross bridge to far towpath. Follow to canal bend & leave cut to reach bend of path. [Griff Hollows]

(N151) Go L 350yds (path from R joins) & under B4113. Join path from R & go 250yds to railway bridge & road.

Seeswood Pool was built to serve a system of lakes and canals around Arbury Hall which connected with the Coventry canal near Marston Junction. Now it is a serene place for the people of Nuneaton, popular with anglers and waterfowl.

At Bermuda Village, apply again our comments on Ansley Common. Here is a quiet and isolated street of the most workaday houses with a double line of lime trees. Look at the tints of the brickwork and the varied cornices, in terracota, red brick and blue. It is really rather nice.

Griff Hollows is a nature reserve and recreation area created from the bed of a disused canal in the valley of the Griff Brook. Over a dense thicket of hazel, bramble, elder and willow are wild cherry, ash and some stag headed oak. This it admirable habitat for many birds and small creatures, and some burned out cars. The district is full of green fragments like this which Nuneaton & Bedworth District Council have formed into a system of pleasant footpaths and cycleways under the title *"Your Green Track"*.

The Coventry Canal runs for 38 miles from the Trent and Mersey Canal near Tamworth to the centre of Coventry, via Haweskbury Junction on the City's edge where it meets the Oxford Canal. There are only 13 locks and it lies in the valley of the low and sluggish River Anker for most of the way, being one of the early canals which followed contours. Its Act of Parliament was passed in 1768 and the first engineer was the pioneer, James Brindley. Hawksbury Junction is also known after its first lock-keeper, as Sutton Stop. Mr Sutton would have been appointed in 1790, when the original 91 mile Oxford Canal was completed. The Oxford was the ultimate winding contour canal; boat people could travel all day in sight of Braunston church. In the 1830s new, straight sections cut many of the loops to reduce the distance by 14 miles.

A prominent feature at Hawkesbury is the derelict pumping house. Its Newcomen-type atmospheric steam engine came

(40)

from Griff Colliery in 1821 and went for preservation to Newcomen's birthplace at Dartmouth in 1963. The graceful 50 foot iron bridge was cast in 1837 when engineers knew how to build graceful cast iron footbridges.

Ansty grew up because of the canal and is now a small village with an attractive jumble of old cottages and new houses. Go and see the two potteries near the bridge. There is a yewey and pleasant churchyard with seats. The church is largely grey sandstone with a pocket Gothic spire designed by Sir Gilbert Scott, though an older red sandstone church survives as the chancel.

*Hawkesbury
Junction*

Coventry Canal
meets Oxford Canal

the disused pumping house

(41)

Ansty

(N147) Put canalside cottages on your L & follow cut 3.5 miles to Greyhound Inn at

Hawkesbury Junction

[(N147X) IF *STARTING HERE* and leaving car at Grange Road canalside car park on the Coventry Arm:

Leave car park & go with cut on your L .3 mile to junction.
NEXT para - (N148) line 4]

(N148) From front door of Greyhound Inn, cross end of Oxford Canal. Turn R & follow towpath of Coventry Canal 1.8 miles to Navigation Inn at

Bulkington Bridge

(N149) From Navigation Inn cross bridge & join towpath. Go under bridge & follow cut 1 mile

- to Marston Junction. Cross over Ashby de la Zouch Canal R & go on 1 mile

- to see isolated yellow brick farm L & Bridge 18.

◄

(S60) Follow towpath to Bridge 18 & cross to far side. Go under bridge & follow canal 1 mile to Marston Junction. Cross over Ashby de la Zouch Canal L & go on 1 mile to Bridge 14 & Navigation Inn,

Bulkington Bridge

(S61) From Navigation Inn cross bridge & join towpath. DON'T GO UNDER BRIDGE & follow cut 1.8 mile to

Hawkesbury Junction

[(S61X) IF *STARTING HERE* and leaving a car at Grange Road canalside car park on the Coventry Arm:

Leave car park & go with cut on your L .3 mile to junction.]

(S62) Cross to Greyhound Inn & pass it on your R to join Oxford Canal. Follow 3.5 miles to Bridge 14 & canalside cottages at

Ansty

►

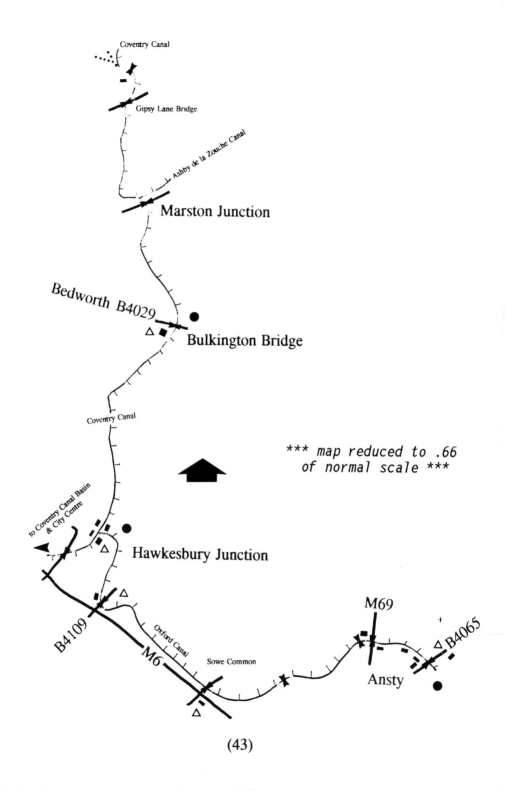

Coventry Canal

Gipsy Lane Bridge

Ashby de la Zouche Canal

Marston Junction

Bedworth B4029

Bulkington Bridge

Coventry Canal

*** map reduced to .66 of normal scale ***

to Coventry Canal Basin & City Centre

Hawkesbury Junction

M69

B4109

Oxford Canal

M6

Sowe Common

Ansty

B4065

(43)

Ansty

(S63) At canalside cottages, go under Bridge 14 & follow cut 400yds to Bridge 16.

****

ALTERNATIVE

The official route cont-
inues on the towpath (S64).
If you want a change from
canal walking you can try
this.

(S63a) From Bridge 16 go R & follow grass track to take stile by L of 2 gates. Follow R hedge to far R field corner & cross stile. ◀

(S63b) Go half L to power pole & gate. Cross fence L of gate to B4029.

(S63c) Go R a few paces & cross road into hedge gap. Follow L hedge .4 mile to corner. Head for brick arch, cross bend of track & climb bank to towpath.

(S63d) Go R .5 mile to near high steel bridge. 100yds before it, climb bank to bridge end & join track. NEXT para (S65)
****

(S64) From Bridge 16 go on 1.5 mile to near high steel bridge. 100yds before it, climb bank to bridge end & join track. ▶

Bridge over the Oxford Canal at Ansty

(44)

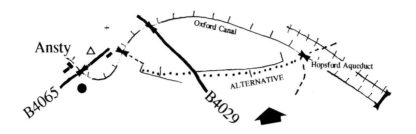

****

ALTERNATIVE

The official route (N146) follows the canal, but there is quite a lot more canal ahead. This field path alternative of about the same distance adds some variety.

(N145a) Go down L of brick wall to track. Walk away from aqueduct to L bend.

(N145b) Go ahead on field path to join R hedge, & follow to B4029.

(N145c) Go R a few paces & cross to gate opposite. Cross fence on its R & go diagonally R to field corner & cross stile. ◄

(N145d) Follow L hedge round 2 corners & take gate/stile ahead. Follow grass track to bridge & join towpath.

(N145e) DON'T GO UNDER BRIDGE - follow towpath to Bridge 14 & cottages at Ansty.

◄ NEXT - para (N147)
****

(N146) From aqueduct follow towpath 1.8 miles to Bridge 14 & canalside cottages at

Ansty ◄

(S65) Go L past house to near farm. (Mobbs Wood Farm) At power pole on R bend, leave track & bear L to take gateway or stile.

(S66) Follow L fence, bearing R across field to take gate R by wood. Follow grass track & take 2 gates.

(S67) Follow R hedge, round field corner, pass lone oak & on 150yds to 2 gateways R.

(S68) Take L gateway & follow R hedge, round 1st field corner to 2nd. Take gateway R, follow L hedge & join track to cross M6.

(S69) Go ahead by L hedge 400yds & take gate L. Go R on fenced track (via gate) to gate & lane by farm.

(S70) Go R, cross railway & follow lane to road junction.

Smeaton Lane

see note re ALTERNATIVE
►

Smeaton Lane

(N140) At T junction on Smeaton Lane, take stem of T. Cross canal & railway to bend & take gate L.

(N141) Go up midfield, take gate & follow fenced track to take gate L. Go R by hedge 400yds & cross M6.

(N142) Follow hard track to field, then follow R hedge to corner gateway. Go L by hedge, round field corner & take next gateway.

(N143) Go L by hedge & round field corner to take gate L, then next gate.

(N144) Follow grass track & take gate. Cross to opposite hedge & go L to gateway. Go ahead to power pole & join track. [Mobbs Wood Farm] Follow to far end of bridge.

(N145) Take gap R & go down bank to towpath. Go ahead .5 mile to brick aqueduct with track below.
◄

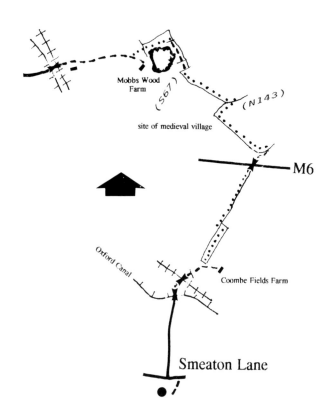

Mobbs Wood
Farm

$(S67)$

$(N143)$

site of medieval village

M6

Oxford Canal

Coombe Fields Farm

Smeaton Lane

Packhorse bridge at Smeaton Lane

(47)

****

ALTERNATIVE

The official Centenary Way route via Coombe Abbey Country Park is described below - para (S71) or (N132). It involves 2.3 miles of road. There are parallel fieldpath alternatives which would avoid 1.25 miles of road, but at the time of writing they are without stiles or waymarks, and are ploughed up annually and not reinstated. Warwickshire County Council has taken no action against the farmer. If these paths are improved an Amendment Slip will be inserted in the back cover.

Because of all this you might prefer our alternative route via Brinklow - para (S70a) or (N131a) This follows pleasant fieldpaths and tracks and the village has many interesting features.

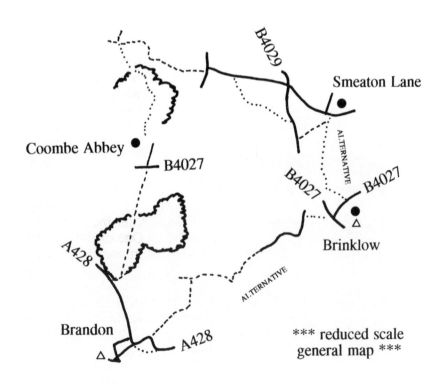

*** reduced scale general map ***

(48)

From Ansty the Oxford Canal sweeps south-east on a bold, curving embankment to the Hopsford Aqueduct. This section is typical of the "new" parts of the Oxford. The dewatered remains of the old line straggle north from near the village and return beyond the Aqueduct. A mile or so from Ansty the CW leaves the canal to cross a lofty bridge and pass Mobbs Wood Farm. Part of the building dates back 400 years and the land belonged to the Coombe Abbey Estate until sold by Lord Craven in 1923. In a meadow beyond the wood broken ground indicates the abandoned village of Upper Smite. The hapless villagers were evicted by the Cistercian monks in about 1150 to make way for sheep. It would probably not console them to know that the site is now registered as an Ancient Monument.

The CW crosses the M6, the Oxford Canal, and a railway, to arrive at Smeaton Lane. From here the official route plods west on lanes; our alternative runs south to Brinklow. We offer a few notes about the main excitements of each.

The *official route* follows a lane past Peter Hall, a farm-house where, peering not too cheekily through an arch, you can glimpse what was, before the Dissolution of the Mona-steries by Henry VIII, a chapel for the monks of Coombe Abbey and, before that, a parish church. A broad track, near a factory (Rolls Royce, strayed from Coventry) leads to a path into Coombe Abbey Country Park.

The Abbey of Cumbe was built by Cistercian monks in 1150, and over the next 150 years became the largest and wealthiest monastery in Warwickshire. After the Dissolution in 1539, the estate had several owners. One of them, John Harrington, built the house in 1581, incorporating bits of the abbey.

There was a link with the Gunpowder Plot, in that James I's daughter, Elizabeth, whom the plotters would probably have put on the throne, was there at the time. The Craven family bought it in 1622, liked it and stayed 300 years.

(49)

Coventry City Council established the park in 1966. The abbey buildings have been bought by a hotel group and the council has built a swanky new Visitor Centre with an immense red brick portico in (very) vaguely classical style. We prefer the children's playground beside it, where we could have had lots of fun had grown ups not kept appearing. Hoopy railings stop the children from escaping, so visitors will be quite safe. The Abbey grounds have ornamental lakes, streams and bridges, with formal gardens and well grown trees: wellingtonia, corsican pine and oak. The main buildings are a disappointing assembly, the view over the lake revealing a very dull and prim classical frontage being nudged by a gabled Victorian bit.

From Coombe Abbey you walk the wooded carriage drive, followed by the Twelve O'Clock Ride. This former carriage road is now a track running between fields and through woods, where you might find muntjac deer the in dense undergrowth.

Brandon has a surprising range of attractive buildings, some timber framed with brick and thatch and some 18th century brick. Look for the jubilantly Victorian terrace with blue diaper patterned brickwork and fretted bargeboards.

Our *alternative* route leaves Smeaton Lane over a fine brick packhorse bridge and follows fieldpaths to Brinklow. The broad main street climbs to the ancient church of St John the Baptist, built in pink and grey sandstone mixed with creamy local limestone. The floor of the nave rises twelve feet from west to east. Above the church rises the hummocky site of the Norman castle of the Mowbrays, all stonework long gone. They built on a Roman fort set to protect the Fosse Way, on the site of an Iron Age fort. Climbing the castle mound and looking south you might see Edge Hill. Castle and church look down on a mini roll call of English pubs - the Dun Cow and the Bull's Head, the White Lion and the Raven. They reflect Brinklow's position on the ancient Fosse Way, and the trade bought by the Oxford Canal.

The grand approach to Coombe Abbey

Timber frame, brick and thatch at Brandon

(51)

(S70a) At T junction, take L arm of T 100yds & take track R. Cross packhorse bridge & go on 80yds to R bend.

(S70b) Cross stile AHEAD (not gate L). Follow L hedge (via 2 gate/stiles) to near end of 3rd field.

(S70c) Cross stile L & go to hedge corner. Bear R & pass L of midfield trees to stile & track. Go R to B4027 at

Brinklow

(S70d) Face Raven Inn & go R to T junction.

(S70e) Go R 50yds, cross road & take path on L of Dun Cow. Follow 70yds, bend R, & go 400yds with gardens R to stile & lane.

(S70f) Go L on metalled surface .6 mile (via bends) to end at gate.

(S70g) Follow track .85 mile (past gateway L & gate L) to R bend with wide & small gates L. Go R 100yds & take track L.

(S70h) Follow .75 mile (via small gate on R bend) to bend on A428. ▶

(N131e) Go R 100yds to fork by gates. Fork L .85 mile to start of lane.

(N131f) Follow .6 mile (past houses L & round L bend) to 1st house R - No.91. Cross stile R.

(N131g) Follow L hedge (at trees enter enclosed path) 400yds to field corner. Take path L to B4027.

(N131h) Go R to junction & L on B4027 to Raven Inn & church at

Brinklow

(N131i) Opposite Raven Inn take Barr Lane (by house No.69) to end of play-ground & cross stile. Cross field passing R of two trees to projecting bramble clump, & cross stile behind.

(N131j) Go R by hedge (via 2 gate/stiles) & cross corner stile to track.

(N131k) Go ahead & cross packhorse bridge to lane. Go L 100yds to T junction at Smeaton Lane.

◀ NEXT para
(N140) on page 46
****

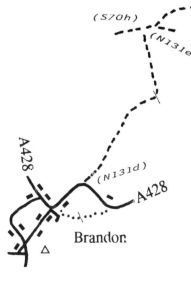

Smeaton Lane

(N131a) From Royal Oak take Avondale Road to bend of A428. Take drive R to bend & cross gate/stile.

(N131b) Go half L to power pole & cross stile. Head for R end of bank & cross stile to A428.

(N131c) CARE: DON'T CROSS HERE. Go L on verge to house. Cross road, go on to L bend & take track R.

(N131d) Follow .75 mile (via small gate & L bend) to T junction of tracks.

(S70c) (N131j)

B4027

Brinklow

B4455

(S70g)

(S70h)

(N131e)

(N131d)

A428

A428

Brandon

(S70i) DON'T CROSS HERE. Go L up verge to house. Cross road, go on to road sign & cross stile R.

(S70j) Go half R to powerpole & cross stile. Head for far end of red houses & take gate/stile.

(S70k) Follow drive down to bend on A428. Go L to crossroads by Royal Oak.
NEXT para (S79) ►
****

(53)

Smeaton Lane

(S71) At T junction take R arm of T 1.3 miles (over B4029) to T junction.

(S72) Go L 75yds & take farm track R. Follow 1 mile (bend R thro farm, then L) to track junction.

(S73) Take kissing gate L, follow L hedge, then fenced path to wood edge gate into Country Park.

(S74) Follow bark path past path R to track by fenced area. Go R to track junction, go L past buildings & pool to path R

(S75) Go R by stream, pass timber bridge R, cross causeway & follow path to Visitor Centre at

Coombe Abbey

(S76) From Visitor Centre go to main carriage drive & follow to B4027.

(S77) Cross & take fenced track 1.3 miles to track junction. Go R to A428.

(S78) Go L on footway .6 mile to Brandon. Take Main Street R & round L bend to crossroads by Royal Oak. ►

(N132) From Royal Oak take Main Street & round R bend to A428.

(N133) Go L .3 mile to Garden Centre & on 100yds to take track R.

(N134) Go 125yds & take gateway L. Follow 1 mile thro woods & fields to B4027. Cross & follow drive to Visitor Centre L,

Coombe Abbey

(N135) Find Visitor Centre door nearest big house & put your back to it. Take path bearing L & cross causeway. Pass timber bridge L & follow stream on L to track.

(N136) Go L between buildings to fork & go R on track to end by fenced area. Take bark path L, pass path L & take wood edge gate.

(N137) Follow fenced path to field. Go R by hedge to kissing gate & track junction.

(N138) Go R 1 mile (thro farm) to road.

(N139) Go L & take lane R 1.3 mile (over B4029) to junction with lane L at

◄Smeaton Lane

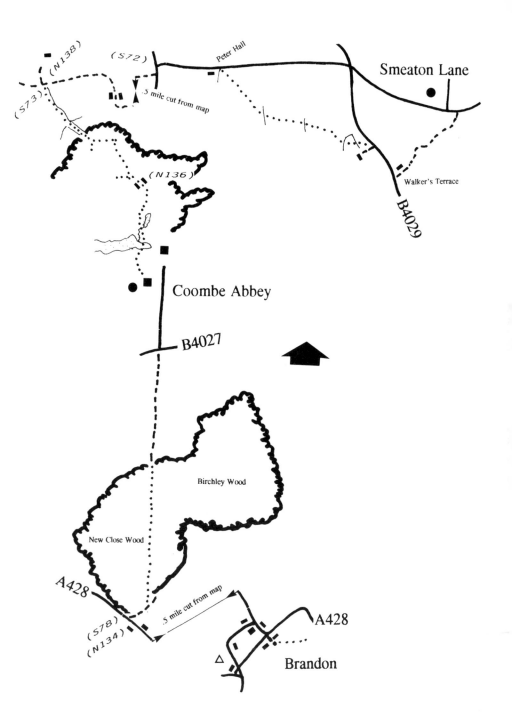

Smeaton Lane

Peter Hall

(N138)

(S72)

(S73)

.5 mile cut from map

(N136)

Walker's Terrace

B4029

Coombe Abbey

B4027

Birchley Wood

New Close Wood

A428

A428

(S78)

(N134)

.5 mile cut from map

Brandon

(55)

(S79) Go under railway, pass castle site & cross River Avon footbridge to take kissing gate R.

(S80) Follow path to church, take kissing gate L & follow drive past school. **(Southbound route runs R down alley on its L.)** Continue on drive to

Wolston

(S81) From War Memorial, cross bridge to school & church gates. Go 25yds & take alley L. Follow to bend of road.

(S82) Take earth track ahead a few paces, then bear R on small path thro trees. Go parallel with houses L, curving R with wooden fence to its corner.

(S83) Go L by fence to next corner & field. Go L 80yds, turn R across field to hedge gap & farm drive.

(S84) Go L 15 paces, turn R & cross field to gap L of oaks. Keep same line to take corner hedge gap.

(S85) Go R 22 paces & turn L to projecting hedge corner. Go with hedge on your L & join fenced path by works to drive & gate.

(N125) Take gap by gate & follow fence. Keep same line past hedge corner & across field to hedge. Go R 22 paces & take gap L.

(N126) Bear R to hedge gap just R of oaks, then keep same line to farm drive.

(N127) Go L 15 paces, turn R & cross field to fence. Go L to fence corner, then R by fence to next corner.

(N128) Go R 7 paces & step up wall L to follow woodland path. Near houses, curve L & go 400yds. Watch for low wooden barriers R & go through them & road.

(N129) Go L & join alley to drive by school. **(North bound route runs L.)** Go R to

Wolston

(N130) From war memorial cross bridge to school & follow drive to its end. Continue on path by church wall & take kissing gate. Go R to gate & road.

(N131) Go L & take footbridge across Avon. Go under railway to crossroads by Royal Oak.

see note re ALTERNATIVE ◄ page 48

(S86) Cross drive & head 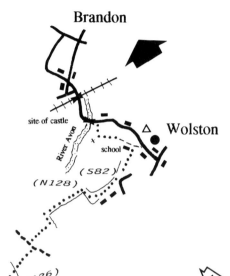 *for far R field corner (parallel with power lines R) to cross footbridge.*

(S87) **LOOK AHEAD** *& note 2 hedges descending hill. Head for bottom of R one, & cross footbridge.*

(S88) Go R a few paces & turn L. Climb with hedge on your L (later follow grass bank) to stile & steps & A45.

(S89) Go R .3 mile on footway & take subway to High Street. Go on to Blacksmith's Arms at

Ryton on Dunsmore
▶

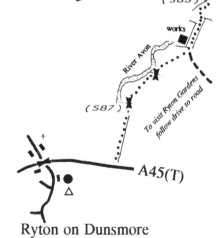

Ryton on Dunsmore

(N122) Face Blacksmith's Arms, go L to A45 & take subway. Go R on A45 footway .3 mile to road sign (Wolston etc). Go on 50 yds to climb steps & stile L.

(N123) Follow grass bank (later R hedge) over crest & down to cross foot- bridge. Go half R to wide hedge gap & cross footbridge.

(N124) Go half R (parallel with power lines L) to works drive & gate ◄

Heading for Wolston, you pass the ruined Brandon Castle and cross the still youthful River Avon on an old stone bridge. For the next twenty miles of the CW the river subtly dominates the landscape, which it largely formed. You follow its valley almost to Kenilworth and meet it again at Warwick, and every brook is a tributary. Ten miles from its source, it is quality Grade B on the National River Authority's A to F scale. A few miles on at Stoneleigh the Sowe flows in from Coventry and the Avon crashes to D. You see it recover to C at Leamington Spa, where it is joined by the River Leam.

Wolston is a large village with a stream running down the main street. There are five small brick bridges, which is more than at Bourton on the Water, even if they are County Council than Cotswold Classical. The buildings are a typical Midlands mixture of timber framing, 18th and 19th century brick, and modern, but they harmonise quite well. A fine church of Norman origin stands beside a long green. By now, the CW walker may have formed an opinion on the question posed by a local tombstone: *"Tell me which is best/ The toilsome journey or the traveller's rest?"*

Long fieldpaths pass near Ryton Gardens, the National Centre for Organic Gardening. Here you can get leaflets, plants, gadgets for making really delicious compost, virtuous vegetables and very good grub. Ryton on Dunsmore itself is wretched, cut in half by a stream of noise called the A45, under which the inhabitants scuttle through a subway. You can see the ancient, towered church of St Leonard and the gaunt and looted Dilke Arms, before negotiating acres of Peugeot cars in the works car park. It doesn't last.

A long and lonely fieldpath leads to Bubbenhall (originally Bubbas Hill), a pleasant village sitting on a low rise by the River Avon. There are many modern houses with a sprinkling of old cottages, some Victorian, some timber framed. The CW passes a pub and the small 13th century church of St Giles, overlooking the Avon. Look at the fine stand of alders by the river; the far bank is a noted resting place for geese.

(58)

Tantara Lodge

A loop of the Avon at Stareton.

(59)

Ryton on Dunsmore

(S90) At Blacksmith's Arms face pub & go R. Take 1st road R (Featherstone Drive) 50yds, to sports field.

(S91) Go L down side of field & take corner gate. Go ahead a few paces & take path L to road. Go R to junction, then L to end of road.

(S92) Go R & take kissing gate. Follow fenced path between car parks .3 mile (via stile & gap in concrete fence) to A423.

(S93) Cross, go L 50yds & take stile R. Go half L to far field corner & cross stile. Follow fenced path to footbridge, stile & field.

(S94) Follow R fence 350 yds (round corner) to cross stile. Go on 100yds to end of hedge L with lone oak.

(S95) Go L 1 mile with hedge on your R (later on track) to bend of road.

(S96) Go ahead 300yds to Malt Shovel Inn at

Bubbenhall
►

Bubbenhall

(N116) Face Malt Shovel & go L 250yds to last bend (NOT END). Take earth track (later grass with hedge on L) 1 mile, to meet wire fence.

(N117) Go R by fence, cross stile, round fence corner & on to cross field corner stile.

(N118) Cross footbridge & follow fenced path to stile & field. Go half L to stile & A423.

(N119) Go L on footway 50yds, cross road & take fenced path. Follow past car parks (at concrete fence take gap & cross stile), & on (via fenced path & small gate) to end of road.

(N120) Go L & take 1st R, pass phone box & take fenced path L to fence corner. Go R & take small gate to sports ground.

(N121) Go R on field edge to road, then R to junction. Go L to Blacksmith's Arms at

Ryton on Dunsmore
◄

(S97) At Malt Shovel Inn, face pub & go R to road junction. Go R to L bend & take lane to church.

(S98) Go thro churchyard & take small gate. Go ahead to far R field corner & cross stile. Cross bridge, follow fenced path & cross stile R. Go ahead to small gate L & lane.

(S99) Go L 200yds to L bend & take house drive R. Follow old quarry edge round corner into fenced path, & round edge of garden to stile & field.

(S100) Go ahead towards shed & cross stile L. Go R by hedge to cross plank & stile R, then L to lane.

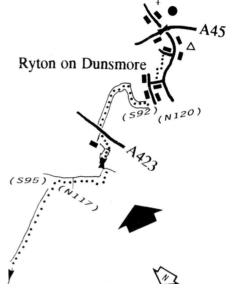

Ryton on Dunsmore

(S92) (N120)

(S95) *(N117)*

A45

A423

(N113) Take gate opposite & go ahead 30yds to cross stile & plank R. Go L up hedge & cross stile L. Go R up hedge & cross stile. Follow fenced path round garden to drive & go R to lane.

(N114) Go L 250yds & take kissing gate R. Go R & cross corner stile to fenced path. Go L, cross footbridge & stile. Head for church & take small gate.

(N115) Pass church & take gate to lane. Go ahead to join road & on to junction. Go L to Malt Shovel Inn at

River Avon

(N114)

(S100)

A445

Bubbenhall

(S101) Cross stile opposite. Go half R (over drive) to far R field corner, & cross stile. Follow R hedge & cross corner stile.

(S102) Go R & take gate. Cross field diagonally & take corner stile. Go R (via stiles) to road.

(S103) Go L 250yds to T junction, then L 350yds to junction. Take road R .7 mile. As it bends & rises watch for Park Farm House L & wall post box R. [Stareton]

(S104) Go R, take small gate & follow path to 2nd gate. Go ahead down woodland path to cross drive & 2 footbridges. [Avon]

(S105) Bear R over CREST of hill & (when in view) 50yds L of old oaks. Cross 2 stiles to B4113.

(S106) Cross, go R 100yds & take small gate L, then on to 2nd gate. Go ahead to L of pond. Bear R to pass double power pole with gizmos & join falling path. Follow (via small gate) & cross footbridge to end of track

Stoneleigh ▶

[(N106X) IF STARTING HERE, go to church & take path to River Sowe footbridge.]

(N107) Cross bridge & take path R (via small gate) to field. Go ahead past far end of bank L to pond. Go L round it & take small gate & 2nd gate to B4113.

(N108) Go R on footway 100 yds & take stile L. Cross 2nd stile. Go half R (50 yds L of old oaks) & down past lone oak. Cross 2 footbridges (River Avon)

(N109) Go ahead (over drive) & follow wood path. Take small gate & go on to gate & road. [Stareton]

(N110) Go L .6 mile to T junction. Go L 350yds to junction. Go R 220yds & cross footbridge R.

(N111) Cross stile, follow R hedge via twin stiles & cross next stile.

(N112) Cross field diagonally & take gate R. Go up a few paces & cross stile L, then follow L hedge & cross next stile. Head for field corner just L of white house & cross drive to stile to lane. ◀

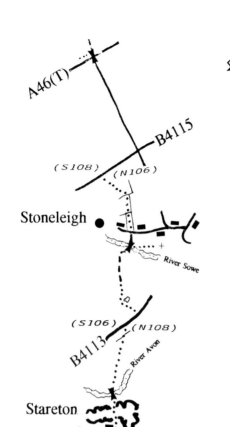

Stoneleigh

[S106X) IF STARTING HERE, go to church & take path to footbridge over River Sowe. If you are south-bound don't cross.]

(S107) From footbridge take track to lane. Cross & take hedged path to cross stile. Follow R hedge & cross ladder stile. Go half L & cross stile R of gates to B4115.

(S108) Go R 300yds to junction. Go L .5 mile to A46. Using L footway, cross bridge & slip road, then take steps L to stile & field. ►

(N105) Go R across bridge & follow road .4 mile to junction. Go R (B4115) 220 yds & pass 1st double gate L to cross stile L.

(N106) Go half L & cross ladder stile to R of field corner. Follow L hedge, cross stile & take hedged path to lane. Take drive opposite to footbridge (River Sowe) at

◄ **Stoneleigh**

(63)

Tantara Lodge confronts you at a T junction, the impressive gatehouse to Stoneleigh Deer Park. A shield shows an eagle with two heads juggling three crowns, a scroll, a book and two pikes. It looks very cross. The estate is now a training centre for Massey Ferguson. Why can't we walk through instead of having to skirt it by road?

At Stareton you join some quite lovely paths. First comes a wood, then two charming little bridges over the Avon, followed by field paths. There is a glimpse to the west of the National Agricultural Centre in the former park of Stoneleigh Abbey, before you cross Motslow Hill to enter Stoneleigh by an attractive footbridge over the River Sowe.

This is a lovely, quiet, little village where the River Sowe flows into the Avon, but in other respects the place is dry. One Sunday morning in 1890 some cyclists from Coventry standing outside the Stoneleigh Arms (now Forsythia Cottage), whistled at Cordelia, daughter of Lord Leigh. He closed the pub and provided that there should never be another. The meadows around the church are preserved by a local trust and the building itself dates back 700 years. It has one of England's finest Norman chancel arches and a filled in Norman arch in the north wall. Wander round and find the row of sandstone almshouses of 1594, the gabled Manor Farmhouse and The Cruck Cottage of old oak timbers.

Fieldpaths and lanes cross Kenilworth Golf Course (once a lonely common) before you follow the Finham Brook through a miniature wooded gorge. A short road walk brings you to Kenilworth High Street.

This is the original Kenilworth, a handsome street of fine brick houses above the church and the Abbey Fields, and leading down via Castle Hill to the famous Castle. The present town centre, half a mile south, is a Victorian impostor that grew up near the railway station, though trains no longer stop here. The church has a great Norman doorway, which probably came from the nearby ruined Priory.

(64)

The Abbey Fields make a pleasant park - its great pool lies below as you climb to Castle Hill. Black and white thatched cottages by the road are known as Little Virginia, from a link with Sir Walter Raleigh and a tale that the first English potatoes were grown here.

The pride of Kenilworth (and about the mid-point of the CW) are the glowing, red cliff faces of the great, ruined castle that was in its time - still is, in a different way - one of England's most impressive buildings. Contsruction spanned 500 years, from the massive 12th century Keep to the Gatehouse converted to a residence in 1650, after the fortress was slighted in the Civil War. A major feature is John of Gaunt's Great Hall from the 14th century. The site is now in the care of English Heritage.

Glowing red cliff faces of Kenilworth Castle

(65)

(S109) Go L by A46 thro 2 fields & cross stile. Go R by fence towards house, take small corner gate to track & follow to R bend.

(S110) Go ahead across stile, field & drive. Pass house on your R & on by R hedge to corner.

(S111) Cross stile to golf course. Go L across fairway & pass thro 2 pine belts. Go ahead with fairways each side, then pass shrub garden on your R to its corner.

(S112) Go R to shed, then L by trees 150yds & take fenced path R. Follow 300yds to road.

(S113) Go R to junction. Go R 50yds, then L (Common Lane) & cross bridge to join path L.

(S114) Follow thro wood .4 mile with brook on your L (via railway arch & past footbridge L) to road.

(S115) Go ahead (past Woodland Drive R) to T junction. Go L to T junction. Go R to A429, then L down to traffic lights.
[Kenilworth] ►

(N99) Take track ahead with BROOK ON YOUR R .3 mile (past mysterious red waterworks, under railway arch & past L forks) to road.

(N100) Go R to junction. Cross road, go R 50yds & take L turn. Go 250yds up to Frythe Close.

(N101) Take fenced path by Close 350yds to golf course. Go L by trees to shed, then R to corner of shrub garden.

(N102) Go L with fairways each side & pass tee R. Keep same line thro 2 pine belts. Go on to projecting hedge corner & cross stile to field.

(N103) Go L by hedge, pass house & cross drive, field & stile. Take track ahead past house & take small gate.

(N104) Go ahead by L fence to A46 & cross stile L. Follow A46 via 2 stiles & take steps to junction. ◄

(S116) Go ahead (High Street) 100yds to old bank L, & take drive L. Pass church L & take path ahead via L bend to Abbey ruins.

(S117) Go thro arch & turn R to end of stone boundary wall. [Abbey Fields] Go ahead with wall on your L & follow rising tarmac path to road. Go down L to B4103 & turn R to Queen & Castle Inn at

Kenilworth Castle

A46(T)

Golf Course

(N101)

Kenilworth Castle

(N96) At Queen & Castle Inn, face pub & go R. Take Castle Hill 200yds to thatched house R & enter park. [Abbey Fields]

(N97) Follow tarmac path down to ruin. Go ahead with ruin on your L & turn L thro arch. Follow path & pass church on your R to High Street.

(N98) Go R to traffic lights. Take A429 opposite 300yds & enter Manor Road R. Follow 200yds & take Tainters Hill L, then Lower Ladyes Hills R to its end.

Kenilworth

A429

A452

(N98)

(S117)

Abbey Fields

B4103

Kenilworth Castle

(67)

(S118) From Queen & Castle Inn, cross main road & take small gate. Skirt castle wall & climb steps to causeway. Go L to road.

(S119) Go R & fork L on track to cross cattle grid. Bear R & take small gate. Follow fenced path to field & keep same line to fence. Go R & cross footbridge by pool.

(S120) Go half L to hedge gap, take gate/stile & on to cross footbridge. Go R by fence to pass farm on your L & take midfence gate. [Oaks Farm]

(S121) Bear L to follow hedge .8 mile (via gate/ stile, corner gap & pool) to stile & Rouncil Lane.

(S122) Go R 40yds & take drive L .3 mile to cross stile L. Go ahead & cross stile. Bear L & cross plank (or bridge) to field corner. [old fish ponds]

(S123) Go R by hedge .5 mile (past 2 stiles L) & cross corner stile into wood. ▶

(N90) Follow wood path to field. Go ahead by R hedge .5 mile (pass 2 stiles R & cross corner stile) to field corner. [Former fish ponds.]

(N91) Go L, cross bridge or plank & take stile. Go ahead to far R corner stile & drive. Go R .3 mile to Rouncil Lane.

(N92) Go R 40yds & cross stile L. Go ahead by R hedge .8 mile (past pool, corner gap & gate/stile) & take midfence gate L of farm. [Oaks Farm]

(N93) Go ahead by R fence & cross footbridge, then on to take gate/stile. Go to far R field corner & cross footbridge.

(N94) Pass pool to end of R fence. Go half L to L of farm & take fenced path to small gate & drive.

(N95) Go L over cattle grid & follow track to junction. Go R & cross footbridge L. Go to Castle gate & take steps R. Skirt Castle walls & take small gate to B4103. ◀

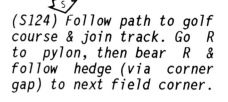

(S124) Follow path to golf course & join track. Go R to pylon, then bear R & follow hedge (via corner gap) to next field corner.

(S125) Go L up hedge & cross stile R. Pass R side of mound, then on to end of far brick wall & take gate/stile. Head for 4th power pole from L & on to farm drive. *[Woodloes Farm]* ►

Kenilworth Castle

Castle Farm

(S120)

(N94)

Oaks Farm

Roundel Lane

Goodrest Farm

(S123)

(N90)

Golf Course

(S125)

Woodloes Farm

(N88) Turn R past nearest power pole, head for L end of small brick wall, & take gate/stile. Go past L side of mound & keep same line to cross stile.

(N89) Go L by hedge, round field corner & take next corner gap. Go to pylon & join track. Follow to next pylon & go L into wood. ◄

From Kenilworth Castle long fieldpaths lead to Warwick. Queen Elizabeth I rode this way on her visits to the Castle, which belonged to her favourite, Robert Dudley, Earl of Leicester. Being relatively dry underfoot, it was known as "the fairest way to Kenilworth".

Warwick was founded in 914 by Ethelfreda, Queen of Mercia and grew up around the great castle by the Avon. The massive building never saw much military action. Despite an attack in 1263 during the Baron's War against Henry III and a siege by Royalists during the Civil War, it took a fire in 1871 to inflict real damage. You will enter or leave the town via Northgate Street, a striking prospect with the 18th century Shire Hall (now County Court) on the west side and the tall, pinnacled tower of St Mary's Church at its south end. Walk around the town; it has fine buildings and quaint ones, beautiful parks, pretty gardens and an imposing market square. By the door of the new Shire Hall is a plaque commemorating the Centenary Way.

St Mary's Church was largely rebuilt in the 18th century, after suffering severe damage in the great fire of 1694 that destroyed 460 of the town's buildings. Fortunately, the 14th century chancel and the 15th century Beauchamp Chapel survived. The chapel contains the tombs of Richard Beauchamp, Earl of Warwick, Henry VI's lieutenant in France in the time of Joan of Arc, and of the Earl of Leicester.

The classic view of the castle is from the bridge carrying Banbury Road (A428) over the Avon. It was built by the Earl of Warwick in 1790 to divert the pounding traffic of the time from a 14th century bridge at the foot of the Castle. The old bridge was later carried away by a flood, but you can still see the abutments.

The three miles from Warwick to Leamington is one of the pleasantest sections of the CW. Leaving Castle Bridge, it follows the River Avon through St Nicholas Park and under a railway and the Grand Union Canal to Portobello Bridge on the A445. Entering Leamington Spa, the CW joins the River Leam through Victoria Park and via the Pump Rooms Gardens to The Parade.

Regency Leamington nicely complements medieval Warwick with more fine buildings and wonderful parks. The CW passes the tourist office at the main gate of the Jephson Gardens, where you can get a useful leaflet, *"A Walk Around Royal Leamington Spa"*. The gardens (named after Dr Henry Jephson, a leading figure in the town's early-19th century expansion as a health spa) lie at the bottom of The Parade, opposite the Royal Pump Rooms of 1814. Overlooking the Leam, their fountains spraying in the sunlight, it is lovely to walk through the rich and varied collection of plants and trees, perhaps with a stop at the Riverside Restaurant.

The CW passes through Newbold Comyn Park which houses a Leisure Centre, where you can swim, lift weights and all sorts of things. The park is kite flying and rushing about terrain, with a golf course and the River Leam flowing along the southern edge. Wander up to the beacon pole for views.

Warwick Castle - the classic view

(71)

(S126) Go L .75 mile to A429. Go R .7 mile (past roundabout, over canal and crest) to railway bridge.

(NB Much of this can be walked on parallel paths & grass in estate R.)

(S127) Take track R by railway (past station side door) .25 mile & take subway L. Follow tarmac path up to road.

(S128) Go L to junction. Bear R & take North Gate Street to St Mary's church,

Warwick

(S129) Face church door & go R. Cross High Street & follow Castle Street to timber framed Oaken's House.

see note re
ALTERNATIVE

(N82) From roundabout follow main road up to traffic lights & take Castle Lane L. At car park bear R to High Street crossroads.

(N83) Take road opposite to St Mary's church,

Warwick

(N84) Face door of St Mary's church & go L to end of street. Cross road bearing R into Cape Road by Police Station. Go down 80yds to L bend & cross to tarmac path.

(N85) Follow down past R fork & under railway. Go R .25 mile [past station side door] to A429

(N86) Go L .7 mile (over crest, over canal & past roundabout) to take lane L. [Much of this can be walked on parallel paths & grass in the estate L.]

(N87) Follow .75 mile (past R fork, over A46, past wood & R fork) to sign by farm gate.

[Woodloes Farm]

****

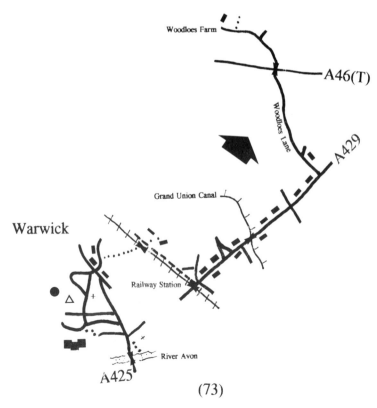

ALTERNATIVE

The offical route continues below, para   (S130).
To visit the Castle:

(S129a) Go R of Oaken's
House & cross road. Take
gate & follow path to
courtyard & entrance.

(S129b) Exit via opposite
gate, go R & take path &
steps down to cutting. Go
L to gate & roundabout.
Cross Mill Street, go
100yds & cross A425 into
park.

NEXT para (S131)
****

****
ALTERNATIVE

The official route   (N82)
goes   on up the road.   To
visit the castle:

(N81a)   Enter   gatehouse
arch & follow cutting to
iron gate. Take steps &
path to gate L & enter
courtyard.

(N81b) Exit via opposite
gate. Bear R & take gate
in wall. Bear L to lane,
take path opposite & join
street to High Street.

NEXT para (N83)
****

Woodloes Farm

A46(T)

Woodloes Lane

A429

Grand Union Canal

Warwick

Railway Station

River Avon

A425

(73)

(S130) Go L of Oaken's House to junction. Go L to A425. DON'T CROSS HERE. Go R past roundabout plus 100yds, then cross road to park. *[NB View of castle from bridge]*

(S131) Bear R to River Avon & follow 1.3 miles (under railway & canal), then round L bend to bridge & A445.

(S132) Go R, fork R & on .25 mile to roundabout. Go R (Princes Drive) .3 mile to end of river bridge.

(S133) Go L under railway to park. Follow River Leam .5 mile (under road bridge) & cross foot-bridge.

(S134) Go to bandstand, then R to Royal Pump Rooms

Leamington Spa ➤

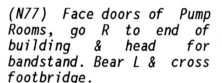

Leamington Spa

(N77) Face doors of Pump Rooms, go R to end of building & head for bandstand. Bear L & cross footbridge.

(N78) Go R by river .5 mile (under road bridge) to railway viaduct & road.

(N79) Go R .3 mile to roundabout. Go L .25 mile & pass junction to far side of bridge.

(N80) Take steps to Avon & follow 1.3 miles (under railway & canal & thro park) to stone road bridge

(N81) Take steps to A425 & cross. *[NB View of castle from bridge.]* Go R past roundabout to stone gatehouse.
◄

Spray and swans at Jephson Gardens, Leamington Spa

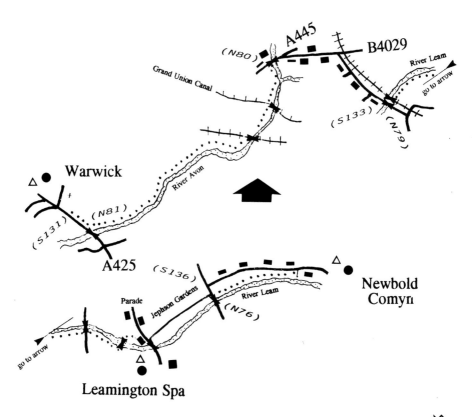

Leamington Spa

(S135) Put your back to Pump Rooms & take gates between white lodges. Go ahead thro Jephson Gardens .3 mile to road.

(S136) Cross & take path opposite. Pass forks R & L & keep same line (thro wood & across grass) to Leisure Centre at

Newbold Comyn
►

Newbold Comyn

(N75) From Leisure Centre take drive out of park. Bear L onto grass & take any path into wood L. Go parallel with river (all paths merge) to road by bridge.

(N76) Take gates opposite. Go ahead thro Jephson Gardens to gates opposite Royal Pump Rooms,

Leamington Spa
◄

Newbold Comyn

*(S137) From Leisure Centre
take drive INTO park .25
mile to gateway after 2nd
adventure playground.*

****

ALTERNATIVE

The official route of the Centenary Way (S138)
(N72) follows the Grand Union Canal Canal for 3
miles if your are southbound, or a further 2 miles
if northbound. It is very attractive but, of
course, level, and some people find canal walking
monotonous. We offer this fieldpath alternative
(with some road) of about 3 miles. Southbound
walkers may wish to know that we join the canal
for the last 1.25 miles. There are fine views over
this rolling landscape, with a pub at Offchurch, if
that counts.

****

Cherry blossom at St Gregory's church, Offchurch

(76)

From Newbold Comyn you have the choice of the official route along the canal or our fieldpath alternative.

The *official* route crosses the River Leam by an unusually long timber footbridge of laminated layers. Soon you are walking the Grand Union Canal which became Britain's first National Canal Trail in 1993. This peaceful, meandering 140 mile off road trek runs from Birmingham's revitalised Gas Street Basin to the classicism of London's Little Venice. Our rural section lies between low hills, its most striking feature the vast arch of the viaduct which used to carry the Leamington Spa - Rugby railway line.

The *alternative* route follows paths which climb above the valley carrying the canal. You pass through the former parkland of Offchurch Bury, a house said to occupy the site of a hunting lodge used by King Offa of Mercia. The village of Offchurch has the Stag's Head and a mainly Norman church. We wanted to go from the Fosse Way through Welsh Road Farm to Ridgeway Lane, but the Right of Way is being diverted. For this edition go down the Fosse Way.

The great blue arch that once carried the Leamington - Rugby railway line over the Grand Union Canal

(77)

****

⌂

(S137a) ᵣrom end of play-ground, go L by hedge to corner of car park & join track. Follow it R 650yds to field with white posts.

(S137b) Go ahead by trees L up to pond. Go L into field, then R past seat to track. Go L to L bend & cross plank R.

(S137c) Go half L & take gateway. Pass a gateway L & follow L hedge to cross corner stile. Go half R to far R field corner & cross footbridge. [River Leam]

(S137d) Go R, cross wide bridge & take gate/stile. Go R & round field corner to join & follow R hedge.

(S137e) Cross drive & on to 2nd drive. Go R 300yds to short fences. Go L to wood corner, then bear R by trees & cross corner gate/stile.

(S137f) Go half R keeping to same contour. Pass fence corner conifers on your R to gate/stile & road. [Offchurch] ◢

(S137g) Go R, pass Stag's ◀Head on your R & follow footway to CROSS lane L. Cross road & go up tarmac ramp to cross stile.

(S137h) Follow R hedge to its corner, pass 10yds L of power pole & climb to top hedge. Cross plank & stile to lane.

(S137i) Go L to road junction. Cross & take stile L of double gates.

(S137j) Go ahead down valley to enter hedge gap & cross railway bridge. Go half R to projecting field corner. Keep same line to end of tall bushes & join green track.

(S137k) Follow to corner at end of sheds. Step L thro fence gap & go UP parallel with farm drive R to gap onto Fosse Way.

(S137l) Go R on verge .4 mile to join canal. Go L 1.25 miles, pass 2 locks to brick arched Bridge 31. NEXT para - (S141) ➤

****

(78)

Newbold Comyn

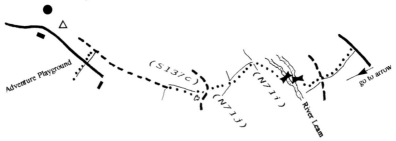

Adventure Playground

(S137c)

(N71j)

(N71i)

River Leam

go to arrow

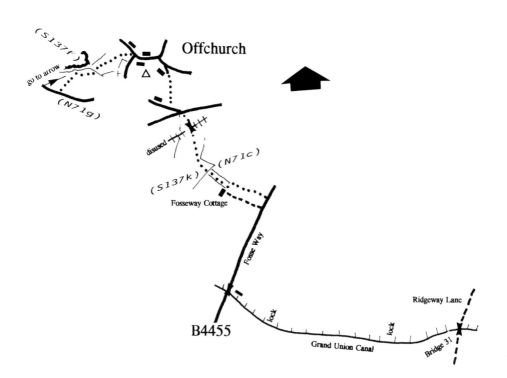

(S137f)

go to arrow

(N71g)

Offchurch

disused

(S137k)

(N71c)

Fosseway Cottage

Fosse Way

B4455

lock

lock

Grand Union Canal

Ridgeway Lane

Bridge 31

ALTERNATIVE
<<< map on previous page <<<

(N71a) At Fosse Way get onto road & go up .4 mile to near crest. After track L (Fosseway Cottage) go 50yds & take gap L.

(N71b) Go parallel with farm track to projecting fence corner R of sheds, & take gap onto green track. Go ahead to its end.

(N71c) Go half R to projecting hedge corner, keep same line to grass mound & cross old railway bridge. Go up valley to power pole & cross stile to road.

(N71d) Take lane opposite to 30mph signs, plus 25 paces, & cross stile R. Cross plank, go down to R of greenhouse & cross corner stile.

(N71e) Go down ramp to lane. DON'T CROSS. Go ahead past lane R, then cross lane to footway. Pass Stag's Head & road L. Follow white wall to gateway L & take gate/stile.

(N71f) Follow L fence to its corner, then head for L edge of wood & take gate/stile. Bear R by trees to wood corner, then bear L midfield to drive.

◄ (N71g) Go R to cedar tree & brick wall. Go L with ditch & hedge on your L, cross drive to field corner & go R by hedge to take gate/stile.

(N71h) Cross vehicle bridge & go R to cross footbridge. Go R to pass 20yds L of far midfield oak & cross midhedge stile

(N71i) Follow R hedge to gaps. Pass gap R & step into gap ahead. Crossfield path is usually clear (IF NOT go at right angle to R hedge) to projecting hedge corner. Cross plank to track.

(N71j) Go L 80yds & take gap R. Pass seat to path. Go L 25 paces, then R by trees to track.

(N71k) Go ahead .35 mile & take gate at corner of car park. Go L to drive & R to Leisure Centre at

Newbold Comyn.
◄NEXT para - (N75)
****

◄ (80)

The route follows the Grand Union Canal to Longhole Bridge and joins Ridgeway Lane. This hedged and rutted track dates from prehistoric times; in wet weather the mud may concern you more than the history. Take a snorkel. The track runs on to Ufton on the A425. The White Hart generously declares that *"absolutely everyone"* is welcome and offers the only game of French Boules we have seen in the Midlands. There is a tea room and a small 13th century church in an imposing position.

Just outside the tiny village, the CW passes through Ufton Fields Nature Reserve, managed by Warwickshire Wildlife Trust for the county council. The 77 acres of ponds and grassland was established in 1972 on ground worked twenty years earlier for limestone; hence the grassed-over spoil ridges - 23 in all. It is noted for six species of orchid, a range of birds including eight species of warbler, siskin, lesser redpoll, water rail and long eared owls. There are also moths, butterflies, dragon flies and damselflies. Sit quietly in the hide and see what comes your way.

A long fieldpath and a track lead to a high brick viaduct over the Leamington Spa - Banbury railway line. When dug in 1852, the cutting was the world's deepest. Thirsts worked up by the vast army of Victorian navvies are said to account for the many pubs in the Harbury.

Harbury is a large and attractive village noted for the fossil-ised remains of a toothy 15ft dinosaur (a macroplata) buried 190 million years ago. It was dug up in 1927 and now grins timelessly in the National History Museum. Some of the buildings are in the soft, creamy local limestone with hints of Cotswold gold, and many in old or new brick. The lofty mill, which now seems to support a henhouse, has a stone base with brick tower. Similarly, the broad 13th century church of All Saints is mainly limestone with a squat tower of brick. The poet Richard Jago was vicar from 1745 to 71. Wander about to see several fine houses and interesting streets of stone buildings.

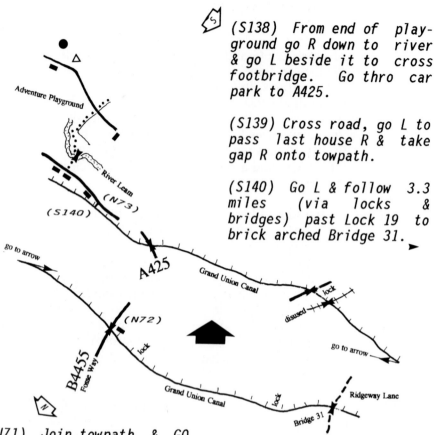

(S138) From end of play-ground go R down to river & go L beside it to cross footbridge. Go thro car park to A425.

(S139) Cross road, go L to pass last house R & take gap R onto towpath.

(S140) Go L & follow 3.3 miles (via locks & bridges) past Lock 19 to brick arched Bridge 31. ►

(N71) Join towpath & GO UNDER BRIDGE. Follow 1.25 miles to wharf & flat concrete bridge. [B4455 – Fosse Way]

see note re ALTERNATIVE page 76

(N72) From Fosse Way concrete bridge follow canal 2 miles (under railway bridge & Bridge 35 (white railings) to Bridge 36. Go on to near house & take gap R to A425. ◄

(N73) Cross & go L .25 mile to house No.162 (Aynho), & enter goal-posts opposite into car park. Go to end & cross footbridge.

(N74) Go L by River Leam to neck of field. Turn R away from river & take rising track to drive. Go L to Leisure Centre at

◄ **Newbold Comyn**

Harbury's mill and viaduct

(83)

(S141) Leave canal & join track. Cross bridge & go 1.25 miles (via green track, hard track & tarmac drive) to A425. Go up L to White Hart at

Ufton

(S142) Take lane by White Hart & round R bend to A425. Cross, go L 100yds past white house R & take gateway R. Pass black shed on your L & cross stile. Follow R hedge & cross stile to Nature Reserve.

(S143) Follow path bearing R (via small gate) to gate & lane. Go R to next bend & cross corner stile L. ▶

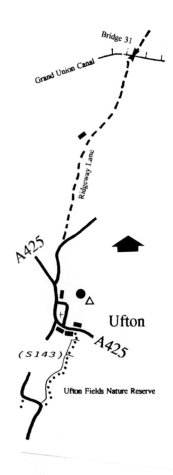

Bridge 31

Grand Union Canal

Ridgeway Lane

A425

Ufton

A425

(S143)

Ufton Fields Nature Reserve

(N67) Follow path via small gate to fork, & go L to stile & field. Follow L hedge & cross stile, then between houses to A425.

(N68) Go L 100yds & take lane R to White Hart,

Ufton

◀

(N69) From front of White Hart go DOWN A425 250yds & take lane R. Follow 350yds & take track L.
[Ridgeway Lane]

(N70) Follow past barn & continue on green lane to Grand Union Canal bridge.
◀

(S144) Go ahead towards R side of white house & cross midfence stile. Follow L hedge (via stiles & past house) to gate & fenced track.

(S145) Follow to 50yds from farm [Bull Ring Farm] & cross stile L. Take hedged path round farm to drive. Go ahead over railway & follow lane to bend of road.

(S146) Go ahead to cross-roads. [Dog Inn] Take road opposite to T junction at Village Hall

Harbury

Harbury

(N63) From Village Hall, take Ivy Lane opposite Follow to crossroads [Dog Inn] & go ahead to bend & junction. Go ahead & cross railway.

(N64) Follow track 50yds to junction. Go ahead but step R onto verge, & join path round farm to stile & track. [Bull Ring Farm]

(N65) Follow track from farm & take gate. Follow R hedge (via stiles & past house) to stile & open field.

(N66) Go ahead parallel with L fence & cross stile near gate to lane bend. Go R to next bend & take small gate L to Nature Reserve.

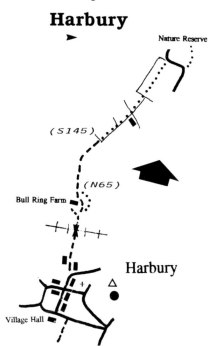

Nature Reserve

(S145)

(N65)

Bull Ring Farm

Harbury

Village Hall

(S147) Face Village Hall, go L 50yds & take track on L of playground to cross stile. Follow R hedge to field corner & cross stile R & plank.

(S148) Bear L to cross end of playing field & take recessed corner stile L. Go R past midfield oak to stile & road.

(S149) Go R 50yds & take gate/stile L. Follow L hedge (via gates/stile) to cross corner stile, then by R hedge to stile & road.

(S150) Go R 150yds & take double gates L. Turn L & follow L hedge .4 mile (via gates) to double white gates & drives.

(S151) Go R 25yds & take gate L to wooded track. Follow to small gate & field. Follow L hedge 1.7 miles (via gates); watch for wood L *[Itchington Holt]* & go on to its corner.

(S152) Go L & follow wood edge round bottom corner with small gate to B4451.

Itchington Holt
▶

Itchington Holt

(N57) At gateway with lane opposite, take gateway. Follow R hedge to wood corner, take small gate & go up to next corner.

(N58) Go R by wood *[Itchington Holt]* & hedge 1.7 miles (via gates), & take wooded track to gate & drive.

(N59) Go R 25yds & take double white gates L. Go with hedge on your R (via gates) .4 mile, pass last house & take gates R to road.

(N60) Go R 150yds & cross stile L. Follow L hedge & cross stile, then by R hedge (via gate/stile) to gate/stile & road.

(N61) Go R 50yds & cross stile L. Pass midfield oak & cross stile to sports field. Go R to L side of house & cross plank & stile.

(N62) Go L by hedge (via stile & track) to road. Go L to Village Hall at

Harbury
◀

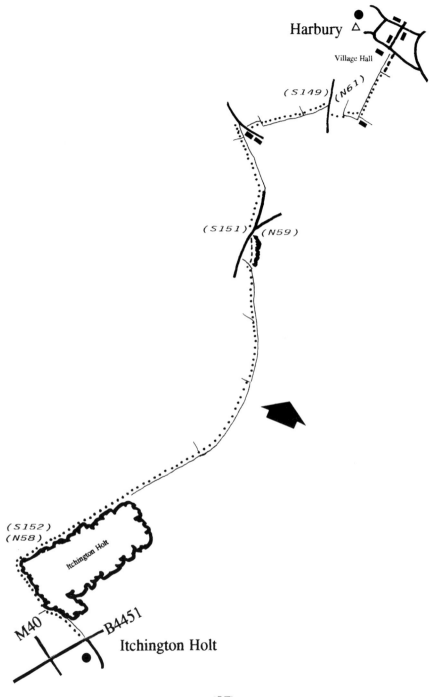

Harbury

Village Hall

(S149) (N61)

(S151) (N59)

(S152)
(N58)

Itchington Holt

M40   B4451   Itchington Holt

(87)

Just south of Harbury the official Centenary Way takes to tarmac for over half a mile. This is pointless and we have ignored it in favour of an excellent fieldpath route.

Warwickshire south of the Avon is known as the Feldon, from the Saxon for field domain. The word suggests a landscape very different from the wooded Forest of Arden north of the river. A 3 mile bridleway crosses a modern Feldon of arable land to the great wood of Itchington Holt, with glimpses of Chesterton windmill to the north-west. Built in 1632 as an observatory for the Peyto family and long outlasting their great house, the windmill has been attributed to the architect Inigo Jones.

Itchington Holt is one of the few woods in the Feldon and a wildlife haven. At its south side just above the modern M40, you descend an old saltway that ran from Droitwich to Priors Marston. It provides a striking view ahead of the Burton Dassett Hills.

From Itchington Holt a footpath and some unavoidable lane walking bring us to tiny Northend, at the foot of the hills. There are just a pub, a few houses and a school. The school was founded by the John Kimble Charity, dating from 1469. Young John was a beggar boy, spurned at Southend, but taken in at Northend. He became a wealthy farmer and the village has benefited ever since.

The lumpy, green tops of the Burton Dassett Hills are now a 100 acre Country Park. These strange contours of bare, cropped sheep pastures cover traces of 19th century iron-stone quarrying and older ridge and furrow field systems. The area is a Site of Special Scientific Interest. The hills are topped by a stone beacon, built - possibly as a windmill - in the late 14th century by a heartless absentee landlord, Sir Edward Belknap. He evicted tenants from the hills to make way for sheep, which with the Black Death, led to the disappearance of Southend village, leaving the 12th century church rather isolated.

All Saints, built on a slope and known as the Cathedral of the Hills, has interesting pre-Reformation chancel arch paintings. It is probably the only church in England still to possess its copy of The Directory of Public Worship (1645), which replaced the Book of Common Prayer during the Civil War and the Commonwealth. Outside its gate is a Holy Well, within a crumbling structure dating from 1840.

From the old stone beacon you can gaze west, past Edge Hill to Meon Hill. Only 14 miles away as the crow flies, it marks the northern tip of the Cotswolds. Magpie Hill nearby is 630 feet high and has a toposcope naming points of interest far and near.

The Burton Dassett Hills, with the topograph on Magpie Hill, and in the blue beyond, the Beacon.

Itchington Holt

(S153) From gateway with lane opposite, take lane. Go .25 mile (round L bend) to stream, & take gap R.

(S154) Follow L ditch & join track. Go on to double gates & take small gate L. Follow L ditch & hedge via small gates to lane.

(S155) Go L 1.25 mile & cross railway to road. Go R .4 mile to Red Lion. [Northend]

(S156) Take lane L of pub to bend. Go ahead past houses & join track to gate/stile & Country Park. Go ahead to rim of valley, then R to Beacon on

Burton Dassett Hills

(S157) From Beacon, head for church (parallel to ridge road). Cross cattle grid & enter churchyard.

(S158) Pass church on your L & cross stone stile. Cross 2 stiles ahead, then bear R to near field corner & cross stile. Go L to cross midhedge stile. ▶

(N50) Head for church tower (via 3 stiles) & cross 4th to churchyard.

(N51) Pass church on your R & take gate. Go ahead to join drive & cross cattle grid. Go ahead on grass parallel with ridge road to Beacon on

Burton Dassett Hills

(N52) From Beacon mound, descend steps & go ahead to rim of valley. Go to bottom & take gate/stile to track.

(N53) Follow past houses to lane bend. [Northend] Go ahead to T junction, then R .4 mile & take lane L.

(N54) Follow 1.25 miles to near wooden fence by M40 & take small gate R.

(N55) Follow R hedge & ditch .5 mile (via small gates & track) to lane.

(N56) Go L .25 mile to B4451.

Itchington Holt ◀

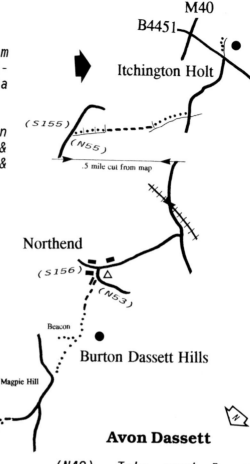

(S159) Go half L to bottom of hollow & cross foot-bridge. Follow L hedge via 1st corner stile to 2nd.

(S160) Go on 150yds, then half R to double gates & cross stile. Go ahead & take gate & lane to

Avon Dassett
►

M40

B4451

Itchington Holt

(S155)

(N55)

.5 mile cut from map

Northend

(S156)

(N53)

Beacon

Burton Dassett Hills

Magpie Hill

(S159)   (N50)

(S160)   (N49)

△
● Avon Dassett

Avon Dassett

(N48) Take road R of Prince Rupert to gate & field. Go ahead & cross stile R of double gates. Keep same line across field corner to join field edge. Follow it to corner & cross stile.

(N49) Follow R hedge (via stile) & cross footbridge. **IF PATH NOT MARKED** go AHEAD (90deg to hedge) & cross midhedge stile.
◄

(91)

Victorian Gothic
in the trees;
St John the Baptist,
Avon Dassett

A high level fieldpath with wide ranging views leads past
wooded Bitham Hill and the grey stonework of Bitham
Hall to Avon Dassett. In this quiet village on the edge
of a plain, that rarity, the village Catholic church, has
outlived its slim spired C of E rival. This latter is uphill,
embowered in trees. It was rebuilt in 1868, but is now in
the care of the Redundant Churches Fund and Stratford upon
Avon District Council, which mows the grass. In the nave
lies a well preserved 13th century tomb, possibly of an
early rector, Hugo.

The *official* route follows a lane to tiny Arlescote. Have
a look at the lovely manor house, which is Tudor, but was
refaced by Inigo Jones in the 17th century, when the flanking
gazebos were added. As boys, the future Charles II and James
II lodged here during the Battle of Edge Hill.

The *alternative* way to Arlescote heads over fields to the
M40, then crosses a bridge. Look east to see 18th century
Farnborough Hall (National Trust) with a nearby village
spire and obelisk, all on high ground.

(92)

Warmington is is a counterpart to Avon Dassett, between the plain and the hills. This is a gorgeous, daydream village where golden houses and the 400 year old Manor camp round a big, blue pond in a large green. In 1086 the Domesday Book recorded 250 inhabitants, but it does not seem to have grown since. For 800 years St Michael's church has perched high over the village. Records say that the churchyard holds the remains of Alexander Gourdin, a Scottish captain killed at the Battle of Edge Hill, Captain Richard Sannes and seven unknown soldiers. Its situation over the road, once the A41, has become almost tranquil since the M40 took most of the traffic that once toiled and snorted up the steep hill.

From the village the alternative route follows a long field-path which winds along the north-eastern flank of Edge Hill, and gives extensive views north over the Feldon. Traces of old ridge and furrow are very noticeable on the hillsides.

The CW climbs steeply out of Arlescote to a crest, passes near the ancient earthwork of Nadbury Camp, then falls abruptly, before rising again to reach Ratley. You must plunge down the steep village street to find the Rose & Crown, view the mellow stone houses and visit the church of St Peter ad Vincula - St Peter in Chains, an unusual dedication. It was built, hampered by the ravages of the Black Death, between 1340 and 1400. At the main gate is an old trough, once used for salting pork, and in the churchyard stands a medieval preaching cross.

On the wooded ridge of Edge Hill the first move is down, down by the Jacob's Ladder steps, then up, up again to the Castle Inn. The crenelated building was constructed in 1750 to mark the spot where Charles I's banner was displayed before the battle and was modelled on St George's Tower at Warwick Castle. The architect was Sanderson Miller, who lived below at Radway Grange. He also designed Hagley Hall in Worcestershire and became well known for follies, of which Hagley has its share.

Avon Dassett

(S161) Face Prince Rupert Inn & go L to road junction by playground.

****
ALTERNATIVE
The official route now follows 1.7 miles of road
- (S162) (N47), which is OK if you are in hurry, but then you could go on your bike. We offer this attractive 3 mile footpath alternative via the pretty village of Warmington.

Avon Dassett

ALTERNATIVE

(S161b) *(N46j)*

M40

(S161c)

B4100

Arlescote

(N46b)

B4100

(S161h)
(N46d)

ALTERNATIVE

Warmington

(S162) At junction by playground go R 1.7 miles (over M40 & B4100) to Arlescote. ▶

(N47) From Arlescote follow road & cross B4100 & M40 to T junction by playground. Go L to Prince Rupert Inn,

◄**Avon Dassett**

(S)

(S161a) Enter playground & cross stile L. Cross field diagonally to corner & take 2 stiles. Keep same line to pass 25yds R of field edge power pole, & cross stile.

(S161b) Go R down field edge to fence & cross stile L. Follow L fence to cross stile & footbridge. **IF PATH MARKED** follow it. IF NOT, follow R hedge 50yds, then bear L towards skyline church & reach M40 at water trough.

(S161c) Go L by M40 & join gravel track. Follow round L bend to cross stile, then M40 bridge.

(S161d) Turn sharp R & cross stile. Follow track by M40 to gate, then L 600 yds to lane. [Warmington]

(S161e) Go L & take School Lane. Take 1st road L to T junction. [Plough Inn] Go L to green, turn R between pond & Manor House, then R up track [Soot Lane] to road. ▲

(S161f) Climb steps L to churchyard. Go L round church & down steps to road junction. Descend B4100 past 2nd junction plus 30yds & cross road to gateway L.

(S161g) Take gate/stile, follow green track across field & take midfence stile by power pole.

(S161h) Go L on field edge to far corner & cross plank. Go L thro hedge & cross stile. Go R by hedge & take small gap.

(S161i) Bear R to R side of bramble patch & go with hedge on your R. Follow nearly to field corner & take gap R. Go L by hedge (past gap L) & take gate.

(S161j) Go ahead bearing slightly L & cross stile L of pond. Follow R hedge & cross corner stile to drive. Go R a few paces, then L to cross recessed stile & ahead to road. Go L & take R bend.
[Arlescote]
NEXT para - (S163) ►
****

(95)

(N46a) *Go R at mark post (just beyond farm track) & cross stile. Go ahead to drive, then R a few paces to cross stile L. Follow L hedge & cross field corner stile.*

(N46b) *Go ahead (bearing a little L) & take gate. Follow R hedge past 1st gap R to enter 2nd. Go L by hedge to corner by bramble patch R. Bear a little R & take gap into field corner.*

(N46c) *Follow L hedge to corner & cross stile. Go R & cross plank. Follow R field edge past 1st stile R & cross 2nd by power pole.*

(N46d) *Follow crossfield path (forks rejoin later) & take gate/stile to B4100*

(N46e) *Cross to footway & go R to 2nd junction. Take steps, go R round church & L past door. Follow path out of churchyard & down to road.*

(N46f) *Take Soot Lane to green & go L between pond & Manor House to road.* [Warmington] *Go L & take Chapel Lane R to T junction. Go R to next junction.*

(N46g) *Go L a few paces & take gate/stile R. Follow track up to M40, then R by it & cross bridge.*

(N46h) *Go sharp L & cross stile to track. Follow via R bend & take gate. Go ahead on field edge 200yds to water trough. Go 90deg R over crest, then bear L down to field corner & cross footbridge.*

(N46i) *Cross stile & go L by fence to cross stile. Go R by hedge 200yds & cross stile L.*

(N46j) *Go half R (25yds L of field edge power pole) & cross midhedge stile. Take 2nd stile, cross field diagonally to play-ground & exit to road. Go L (past lane L) to Prince Rupert Inn, Avon Dassett.*

◄ *NEXT para - (N48)*

****

Dreamy Warmington

Castle Inn, Edgehill

(97)

(S163) Follow road to Pond Farm drive, then on 75yds to cross steel fence L.

(S164) Go ahead & cross stile. Go up by L hedge to field top. Go R to power pole, then L to stile & B4086.

(S165) Cross into hedge gap & go ahead & down to cross footbridge. Head for top L field corner & cross stile.

(S166) Cross CREST of field & (when in view) head for middle of conifers to reach project-ing wall corner. Go ahead via gate & track to road junction at

Ratley ➤

(N44) From junction at top of High Street, take track. Take gate & go with wall on your R to its corner. Cross CREST of field to far L corner & take stile.

(N45) **SIGHT FIELD-BOTTOM TREES**, a pair & one. Head 25 yds L of lone tree & cross bridge. Head for field top power pole & take gap to B4086.

(N46) Cross stile opposite & go ahead to power pole. Go R to field edge & down by hedge to cross corner stile. Go ahead & cross fence to road. Go R into Arlescote & round L bend plus 50yds to farm track L. DON'T ENTER.

see note re
ALTERNATIVE
◄ page 94

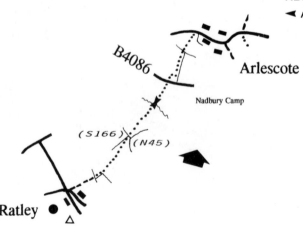

Ratley

(S167) From junction at top of High Street, take Edgehill/Kineton road 400 yds to T junction.

(S168) Bear L across road & take steps [Jacob's Ladder] to track at bottom of edge. Go L 600 yds (L at fork) & climb edge to tower [Castle Inn].

(S169) Just before tower go R down railed path to bottom path. Go L .6 mile (via steps up & steps down) to meet rising track. [King John's Lane]

(S170) Go up 25yds & take path R. Follow by fence .4 mile, then down to lane.

(S171) Go up, pass track R & take path R by farm wall. Follow .5 mile (at short mark post, pass path R) to road at

Sun Rising Hill ►

Sun Rising Hill

[(N38X) IF STARTING HERE: From layby pass phone box to drive L. DON'T ENTER]

(N39) Take narrow path opposite drive .5 mile to farm & lane.

(N40) Go down L 25yds to power pole & join path R. Follow .4 mile to falling track. (King John's Lane)

(N41) Go down 25yds & take path R (via steps) to fork. Go L down steps .3 mile to path junction with stile L.

(N42) Take railed path up R to tower. Go down L .35 mile (joins track) to path junction & small gate L.

(N43) Take steps R up to road. Take road opposite to road junction at

Ratley ◄

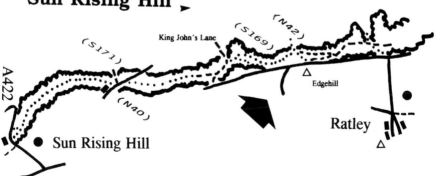

Sun Rising Hill

Middle Tysoe

[(S171X) IF STARTING here: From layby pass phone box & take drive L.]

(S172) Take drive ahead & cross gate/stile R. At junction go L (past falling track R) & take gate. Follow L fence & take gate

(S173) Follow wood edge path 400yds, then take falling track thro trees to bottom gate.

(S174) Head for bottom L field corner & take gate. Go ahead 100 yds & cross stile L. Cross field diagonally to take gap & stepping stones.

(S175) Follow R hedge & cross stile. Go on 2 fields to gap.

(S176) Cross field to tree L of distant church & join field edge. Follow R hedge to corner gap. Go half R to corner gate/stile & road. Go L past church to Peacock Inn

Middle Tysoe ◄

(N35) Face Peacock Inn, go R past church to 30mph signs & cross gate/stile R

(N36) Go half L to projecting hedge corner. Go with hedge on your L past tree plus 25yds. Bear R across field & enter hedge gap. Follow L hedge (via stile) to stepping stones & take gap.

(N37) Cross field diagonally & take corner stile. Go R & take gate. Go half L by shallow ditch to field corner & take gate.

(N38) Follow woodland track up to top fence. Go L & take gate. Follow R fence round edge & take gate. Go ahead to drive, go R (via gate/stile) to junction, & L to A422 at

Sun Rising Hill ◄

see note re ALTERNATIVE

A422

(S176)

(N37)

(S174)

Sun Rising Hill

△ +

Middle Tysoe

(100)

Views from Edge Hill are best found when the trees are bare, and the only unobstructed outlook is just south of Sun Rising Hill. When the Battle of Edge Hill took place on the lovely Sunday afternoon of 23rd October 1642, the present woods did not exist and the area was largely grassland. This was the first major set-to of the English Civil War, when 14,000 Royalist troops were led by the king and his dashing young nephew, Prince Rupert, and the 10,000 Parliamentarians on the plain below by the Earl of Essex. About 1,200 combatants were killed, and if any who survived were alive today they would still be arguing about which side won. Ironically, the battlefield is now Ministry of Defence land and out of bounds to the public. A memorial stands beside the B4086, a mile east of Kineton.

In January 1643 the first report appeared of a re-enactment of the Battle of Edge Hill. Shepherds, travellers and some local people claimed to have seen it take place in the sky over a period of three hours. Similar reports have been made many times by many people, including a commission sent later in 1643 by the King. Sightings have been reported ever since, including the 1940s, 50s, 60s and 70s. You can read more in *Midlands Ghosts & Hauntings* published by QuercuS. [Ahem! yes - John Roberts's other imprint actually; same address etc as Walkways.]

A long, wooded path leads to Sun Rising Hill, with its magnificent outlook over the Vale of the Red Horse. This great beast was carved at an early, indeterminate date on the hillside near Tysoe, but destroyed in 1798 when the fields were enclosed. It may have had an ancient link with the distant Vale of the White Horse in Berkshire. Charles II is said to have breakfasted at Sunrising House on the morning of the battle.

Descending from Edge Hill, the CW crosses level fields to Middle Tysoe. You can see the sails of the early 18th century Compton Wynyates' windmill, which was restored by the Lord of the Manor, the Marquis of Northampton, in the 1970s.

****

ALTERNATIVE

The official route follows the main road for .6 mile - paras (S177) and (N31). Our version cuts this to 400yds.

(S176a) Face Peacock Inn, go L to War Memorial & fork R (Oxhill) to T junction. Go R past Windmill Way & take path L.

(S176b) Follow to end & cross stile. Cross field diagonally & take stile. Go thro thicket to field & go ahead, bearing L to take gateway.

(S176c) Pass green track R & follow R hedge to cross corner stile. Go ahead, bearing L to cross stile 60 yds L of field corner.

(S176d) Go to far L field corner & cross stream & stile.
NEXT para (S180) ►
****

(N30a) From stream go ahead, bearing L to cross midhedge stile. Go to far L field corner & cross stile. Follow L hedge & take gap.

(N30b) Go to far L field corner & thro thicket to cross stile. Cross field diagonally & take stile 25yds R of corner. Follow path to lane.

(N30c) Go R & take lane L to main street. Go L to Peacock Inn, Middle Tysoe.
◄ NEXT para (N35)
****

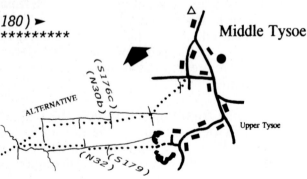

(S177) Face Peacock Inn & go L (past roads R and L) to junction on bend. Go R (Shipston) .25 mile (past roads R & L) to sharp L bend by stone pillared gateway.

(S178) Enter gateway, go ahead between walls & follow woodland path to small gate & field. Go ahead to far R field corner & take gate.

(S179) Follow R hedge 150 yds & take gate R. Go L by hedge, bearing R to take gate. Follow L hedge to cross stream & stile.➤

(N31) From stream follow R hedge & take gate. Continue to far R field corner & take gate R.

(N32) Go L by hedge & take corner gate. Go ahead, bearing R to take gate in centre of wood.

(N33) Follow woodland path then gravel drive, to gateway & road.

(N34) Go L .6 mile (via L bend) to Peacock Inn at

Middle Tysoe
◄

Church of the Assumption, Middle Tysoe

(S180) Go ahead (drawing closer to L hedge) & cross stile. Go ahead midfield, enter gap & follow fenced track to field. Follow R hedge to water troughs, plus 30 paces.

(S181) Bear L & cross mid-hedge footbridge. Go up to oak in top hedge. Go R by hedge 200yds & cross stile L.

(S182) Go half R to far corner of garden *[Kirby Farm]* Go down edge of farm to steel barn, then bear L & take field bottom gate. KEEP SAME LINE to cross stile & footbridge.

(S183) Go L & cross stile. Go R to wide hedge gap, then half L to R of middle red house & cross stile. Go ahead to lane & R to Royal Oak at

Whatcote
►

Whatcote

(N27) Take lane opposite Royal Oak & go L (Rowlands Way) to cross stile. Go half R thro corner gap & follow L hedge to cross corner stile.

(N28) Follow R hedge to cross footbridge & stile. Cross fields diagonally (via corner gap) to far end of green steel barn, then beside farm to corner of garden. *[Kirby Farm]* Bear L to just R of steel barn & cross stile.

(N29) Go R by hedge 200yds to 2nd oak. Go half L to cross midhedge footbridge. Keep same line to projecting hedge corner. Go with hedge on your L, then on fenced track to its end.

(N30) Go ahead & cross stile 25yds L of field corner. Keep same line to tree gap & cross stile & stream. ◄

see note re ALTERNATIVE

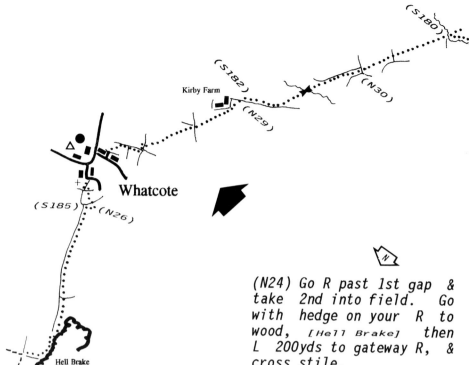

Kirby Farm

Whatcote

(S185) (N26)

Hell Brake

(N)

(N24) Go R past 1st gap & take 2nd into field. Go with hedge on your R to wood, [Hell Brake] then L 200yds to gateway R, & cross stile.

(N25) Go L .6 mile (via 2 stiles), round field corner plus 25yds & cross gate/stile L.

(N26) Go to top L field corner & cross stile. Take 2nd stile & gate to churchyard. Exit to road & go L to T junction. Go R to Royal Oak at

Whatcote
◄

(S)

Whatcote

(S184) Face Royal Oak & go L. Take Church Lane L & enter churchyard. Go L & take small gate, then stile. Go R (via stile) & cross field bottom gate/stile.

(S185) Go R to field corner. Follow hedge .6 mile (via 2 stiles) to near wood [Hell Brake], & cross stile R. ►

Tysoe comes in three parts - Lower, Middle and Upper. Lower (or Temple) Tysoe, once owned by the Knights Templars, is off the CW. At Middle (or Church) Tysoe we pass a fine, large church in a pleasant green churchyard. Within the nave, supported by Norman columns, stone faces peer down and there are ancient monuments and brasses. This is one of the bigger villages on the CW, with the Peacock Inn, a Post Office, two general stores, a butcher, hairdresser, police station, village hall and fire station, suggesting a lively social scene with much crime and arson. The older houses are in sombre ginger and brown variants of the same stone you have seen since Avon Dassett, but there are buildings from all periods and many modern houses. They make the road to Upper Tysoe seem rather suburban, and we recommend our fieldpath alternative to the official route.

Level, lowland fields with just one rise lead to tiny Whatcote. Most buildings in the village are modern, though you must look carefully to tell. However, the Royal Oak may be the oldest inn in the county, having (it's said) been established 800 years ago as a shelter for workmen building the village church. Surprisingly for this remote rural place, St Peter's church was badly damaged in World War II by a bomb from a German plane returning from a raid on Birmingham. One rector was a descendant and namesake of Sanderson Miller, whom we met at Edge Hill. Another, John Davenport, served for 71 years from 1597 and lived to be 101. The Old Allotments Round Walk was inaugurated in 1994 and includes part of the CW route. A leaflet is on sale.

Leaving the churchyard you cross a stile erected in May 1995 by the Whatcote Village Association. Inscribed in the concrete step is the intriguing name - The Devil's Toenails. We have not tried to find out what it means. However - a field edge path climbs from the village to a wood, Hell Brake, and up beside it to the plateau of Idlicote Hill. Is the wood eerie, or does it seem so because we are told that it is haunted? Does the Devil come here for chiropody?

From the plateau you can look across the Vale of the Red Horse to the Burton Dassett Hills and Edge Hill. To the south you may see the final upland on the CW, Meon Hill, at the edge of the Cotswolds. You may not be able to reconcile the CW route over Idlicote Hill with your OS map because it has been diverted to the the more angular path which we describe. The process caused much ill will because the new route connived at years of flagrant obstruction by the landowner.

The high fences around some of the woods are to keep out deer. Tread lightly, scan the ground for their "slots", or hoofprints, and watch. On one day we saw three groups of fallow deer. The first was of eight, one being dark and the others pale cream or white. The second group of four had three dark and one cream. The third was a group of four, of which three were white. All seemed to be does or juvenile bucks. In other parts of the Midlands, especially Cannock Chase and the Wyre Forest, we seem to see many more of the dark variety. Deer experts, please comment?

A place to rest. Whatcote

(S186) Go L by wood to field corner, then R up hedge & take corner gap. Take track L to Idlicote Hill Farm, then track L to its end.

(S187) Go R by hedge to sharp angle of high fence. Take track R .6 mile
- past wind pump & down to high fence corner L,
- L by wood, thro hedge gap & R to meet wood.
[Hill Clumps]

(S188) Go L down wood edge (past red brick wall & pond) to wood corner by concete water trough.

(S189) Go R 35 paces then L on track to field edge. Go R down track to small wood & take hedge gap L. Go R round field corner (past gateway R) & down to track.

(N20) Go thro gateway & L up field edge. Round top corner & go 25yds to take gap L. Take track R 250 yds to wide gap R. Take track L 20yds to track by wood. [Hill Clumps]

(N21) Go R & round wood corner. Pass pond & red brick wall plus 100yds, up to wide hedge gap ahead.

(N22) Take track R .6 mile
- by L hedge to wood,
- L to high fence corner,
- up R past wind pump &
- R by high fence
to sharp fence corner.

(N23) Go L by fence 200yds & take track L to Idlicote Hill Farm. Take track R to sharp L bend by oak.

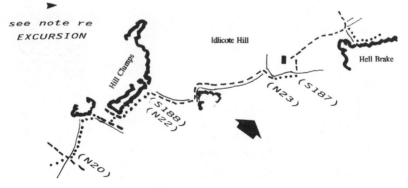

see note re EXCURSION

You can go straight to Honington, or take the Excursion to Shipston on Stour. This little town is mainly Georgian brick; a genial jumble of small streets, lanes and alleys, which open onto an impressive central square. Here are buildings of every age and style, in timber framing, brick and limestone. The facades are a riot and all at different heights, but it makes a chaotic sort of harmony. Shipston coined money from the Cotswold wool trade and a sheep market, but has not expanded much since the 18th century.

Honington is a restrained and somnolent village of wide verges and discreet houses, mainly in pale limestone. All Saints church is a baroque contrast. Apart from a 13th century tower it was built about 1680 in classical style. There are amazing marble monuments: Joseph Townsend's (1763), includes what Arthur Mee called *"perhaps the most unpleasant cherub in all England"*, and the late bewigged Parkers, father and son, are seen walking, talking and looking lively enough to step down the aisle.

The CW crosses the River Stour twice. The Shipston Excursion does so by the most tumbledown, brick, farm bridge. Honington has a golden classical bridge, built when the road was cut through the parkland of Honington Hall.

Honington's golden bridge over the River Stour

(109)

EXCURSION

The main route continues via paras - (S190) and (N19). Below is a loop visiting Shipston on Stour.

(S189a) Go R thro gateway & take gate/stile L. Go half R to bottom of 3 hedge-trees & cross mid-hedge stile.

(S189b) Cross field diagonally & take stile R of corner. Go half L to bottom corner gap (?stile) & lane. [Fell Mill Lane]

(S189c) Go L over bridge & cross stile R. Go half L over crest & cross footbridge. Follow River Stour 50yds & cross brick bridge.

(S189d) Follow R field edge (via gate/stile) to tarmac drive & follow (via gate) to A3400. Go L on footway into

Shipston on Stour ◀

(S189e) From town centre ◀take A3400 (Stratford). Pass hospital R, go on past octagonal yellow brick tollhouse L & take gateway R (Springhill).

(S189f) Take gate & follow L fence over crest (via gate/stile) to cross brick bridge.

(S189g) Go L by river 50yds & cross footbridge. Go half L over crest to field corner stile & lane.

(S189h) Go L .6 mile to T junction. [Honington].
    NEXT para (S191) ►
****

(S190) Take gateway & follow wide track (via gate & stile) to gap & lane. Go R to T junction. [Honington] ►

(N18a) From buff brick house, follow lane .6 mile to bottom of dip. Cross bridge over stream and go R to cross stile. Go half L over crest & cross footbridge. Follow River Stour 50 yds & cross brick bridge.

(N18b) Follow R field edge (via gate/stile) to tarmac drive. Go ahead (via gate) to A3400. Go L into

Shipston on Stour

(N18c) From town centre take A3400 (Stratford etc) to hospital R. Go on past octagonal yellow brick tollhouse L & take gateway R (Springhill).◄

(N18d) Take gate & follow ◄L fence (via gate/stile) over crest to cross brick bridge.

(N18e) Go L by river 50yds & cross footbridge. Go half L over crest to field corner stile & lane.

(N18f) Go L over bridge & take hedge gap (?stile) R. Go half L & cross midhedge stile. Cross field diagonally & take corner stile.

(N18g) Go half L to top R field corner gate/stile & join track.

◄ NEXT - para (N20)
****

Honington

Fell Mill Lane

River Stour

(S190)

(N20)

A3400

(S189a)

see note re
EXCURSION
page 110

Shipston on Stour

(N19)► From buff brick house take hedge gap L. Follow track by R hedge (via gate & stile) & over crest up to gateway with gate/stile R. next para
◄ (N20) on page 108

(S191) Go L thro village
[To see church take lane
R] .5 mile to A3400.

(S192) Go R on footway .6
mile. Look for house L by
Z bend sign & go on to
next gate L.

****

ALTERNATIVE

The official 4.25 mile route between Honington and
Ilmington includes 3.3 miles of road walking -
para (S193) or (N14). Our 4.5 mile alternative via
Darlingscott is almost all on pleasant fieldpaths
with only an unavoidable 1.2 miles of road. The two
routes meet briefly at the A429 Fosse Way.

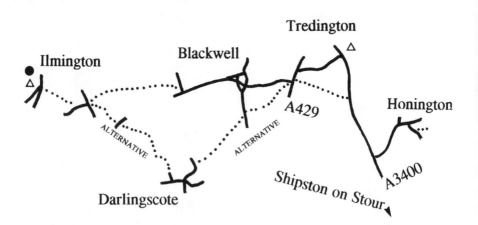

*** reduced scale general map ***

(S192a) Take gate L, go half R to big willow & take double gates. Take next gates R, pass gate L & follow L hedge (via gate) to crest.

(S192b) Take gap & follow R hedge, round bottom field corner & cross stile to A429. Cross to lane.

(S192c) Go a few paces & take gate L, then stile R. Go half L passing midfield power pole on R & cross fences & plank to track.

(S192d) Go R & take gate. Go L by hedge down to field corner & cross fence L. Go thro thicket & cross fence to field corner. Go ahead a few paces & take footbridge R.

(S192e) Go ahead over crest (via gate) & take gate to road.

(S192f) Take gate opposite & go half L to field corner. Ignore gap L & cross plank & stile. Go ahead & take corner gate.

(S192g) Keep same line via ◄midfence stile & pass projecting hedge corner on your R to cross stile. Follow fenced path to lane

(S192h) Go L 400yds to cross roads. Go R thro village [Darlingscote] & take Potters Lane R.

(S192i) Follow to end & take path past stone house to cross plank & stile. Go ahead & IF PRESENT cross midhedge stile. IF NOT, go to far L field corner & take gate.

(S192j) Cross field to take gate 100yds R of L field corner. Go half L to cross midhedge stile & slab. Go half L to mid-hedge stile & lane.

(S192k) Take gap opposite, go ahead to 3 trees & cross fence. Go ahead to take hedge gap & cross ditch. Cross field diagon-ally to corner stile & road.

NEXT - para (S197) ►
****

(113)

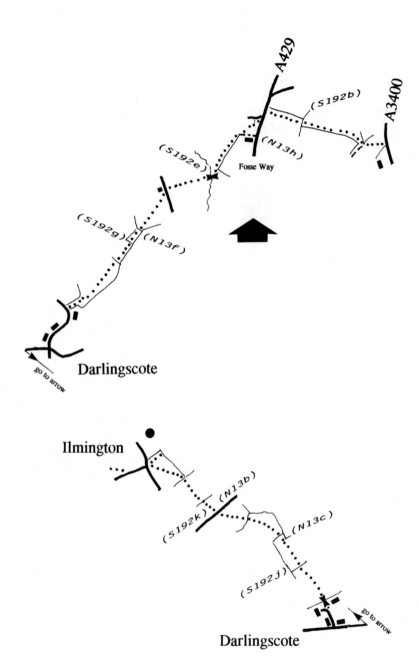

A429

A3400

(S192b)

(N13h)

(S192e)

Fosse Way

(S192g)

(N13f)

go to arrow

Darlingscote

Ilmington

(N13b)

(N13c)

(S192k)

(S192j)

go to arrow

Darlingscote

(N13a) From field corner stile, cross field diagonally, take corner gap & cross ditch. Go ahead to 3 trees & cross fence beneath. Keep same line to gap & lane.

(N13b) Cross stile opposite. Go half L to field corner & cross slab & stile. Again go half L to field corner & take R of 2 gates.

(N13c) Go ahead & **IF PRESENT** cross midhedge stile. **IF NOT** bear R & take field corner gate. Go to R side of stone house & cross stile & plank. Follow path then road to main road. *(Darlingscote)*

(N13d) Go L 200yds to crossroads & take lane L. Follow 400yds, pass gate of 2nd house R to end of garden, & cross recessed stile R.

(N13e) Follow fenced path to stile & field. Follow L hedge to its corner, then keep same line (via midfence stile & corner gateway) to cross midhedge stile & plank.

(N13f) Go half L to shed & take gate to road. Take gate opposite, go ahead over crest (via gate) & down to cross footbridge L of bottom gate.

(N13g) Go L to field corner & cross fence. Go through thicket & cross fence. Go R up hedge & take corner gate to track.

(N13h) Go 20 paces to cross fences & plank L. Go half R & cross corner stile. Take gate to lane & go R to A429. *[Fosse Way]*

(N13i) Go L a few paces & cross road to take stile. Follow L hedge to crest & take gap. Go down with hedge on your R (via gate) & take 2 sets of double gates. Go half L to corner gate & A3400.

(N13j) Cross to footway. Go R .6 mile & take lane L
NEXT - para (N18) ➤
****

The *official* route passes through two villages to reach Ilmington. Tredington's twisting lanes are lined with lovely old cottages and its church includes Saxon work. Look for two doorways above the arcades, perhaps indicating that the building was a refuge from Danish invaders. The tall white spire dominates the lower ground of the Stour valley and can be seen for miles.

The hamlet of Blackwell is a cluster of houses round a small network of lanes. The buildings are very mixed, with rich orange stone and brick - some houses have both, and roofs thatched or tiled. There is a splendid old barn - Blackwell Grange, with a steep thatched roof over brick walls with stone patches. Pleasant enough; nothing to detain you.

The *alternative* route passes through just one hamlet in a level patchwork of green and brown fields. Long lanes run between hedgerows and there are odd, small orchards near the villages, but few trees and no woods. To the east, south and west are modest but definite hills, such as the one on which Tredington stands. The Cotswolds are near.

Darlingscote is a small straggle of stone and brick houses. It was once on the Great Western Railway's line between Moreton in Marsh and Shipston on Stour, and before that on the horse drawn Central Junction Railway from Stratford to Moreton. Today you would not get a bus. Just before the village crossroads you pass the stone built Darlingscote House. A sundial on the wall is dated 1621 and a Sun Assurance firemark shows that the property was insured by that office in the days when they all ran their own fire brigades. You may weigh up the chances of the Shipston appliance arriving in time to do much good.

Ilmington spreads spaciously round a big sloping green with about half the houses on the level and the rest on the foot of a mighty hill, for this is the very edge of the Cotswolds. Ginger and cream stone cottages are mixed with those of red brick, and the roofs vary between tile, slate and thatch. In the late 19th century it briefly became a minor spa, when visitors drank the waters of its chalybeate spring. We pass between the 16th century Manor House and the site of its former fish ponds to reach the churchyard.

The cruciform St Mary the Virgin is entered by a Norman doorway. Squatting next to it is the tomb of James Sanson, looking like a bad tempered wedding cake ringed with mean iron railings, and the gravestone of a parishioner who died at 106 years, 9 months and 11 days. That of Sam Bennet, Ilmington's famous folk dancer and fiddler, lies behind the wall opposite the porch.

Beyond the church, the CW passes the yard of a hurdle maker. Here we have taken our final liberty with the official route, which makes a pointless detour by road. We ignore it and send you up a grassy short cut. The CW follows hilly footpaths with a vast outlook north across the Feldon, or east to Edge Hill and the Burton Dassett Hills. In a hollow lies the chalybeate spring, a pool shown on the OS map as Newfoundland Well. Ilmington Downs at nearly 800 feet and topped by radio masts rise to the south, but the CW turns its back on them for half a mile of road walking and some level fieldpaths, before it starts climbing again.

You cross a shoulder of Meon Hill where you have more fine views, not least of which is the sight of the 127ft spire of Lower Quinton church. The hill was the scene of the famous unsolved "witchcraft" murder on St Valentine's Day 1945, when a 76 year old farm labourer was found impaled on his pitchfork in circumstances suggesting satanic rites. There is also something about a black dog with eyes like glowing coals ... you know the sort of thing. Anyway, if you clap eyes on it, you're doomed.

It is probably as well that the Centenary Way ends on the large green at Upper Quinton, and again meets the Heart of England Way.

(S193) From gate L go on up A3400 to junction. [Go R for Tredington] Take Blackwell Road L to A429. [Fosse Way] Go L 170yds & take lane R.

(S194) Follow .6 mile, over 2 crossroads & thro village to Y junction by thatched barn. [Blackwell Grange]

(S195) Go ahead 400yds & take lane R. Follow 100yds & take gate/stile L.

(S196) Follow L hedge & cross stile ahead. Cross field diagonally & cross corner stile. Follow R hedge (via stiles & gate/ stile) to stile & road.

(S197) Take lane ahead 200 yds & enter hedge gap R. **ON CREST AHEAD SEE 3 POWER POLES.** Head for middle one, then to far R field corner. Take gap & track to road at Howard Arms,

Ilmington

(N14) From field corner stile follow L hedge (via gate/stile & stiles) to stile near pylon. Ignore waymark & cross field diagonally to take stile. Follow R hedge to gate/ stile & lane.

(N15) Go R to junction, go L 400yds to fork by Blackwell Grange.

(N16) Fork R thro Blackwell & follow lane .5 mile (over 2 crossroads) to A429. [Fosse Way]

(N17) Go L 170yds & take lane R. Follow to A3400. [Go ahead for Tredington] Go R 1 mile & take lane L.

(N18) Follow .5 mile thro Honington [Fork L to see church] & take Fell Mill Lane R. Follow 150yds to buff BRICK house.

next para
(N19) on page 111

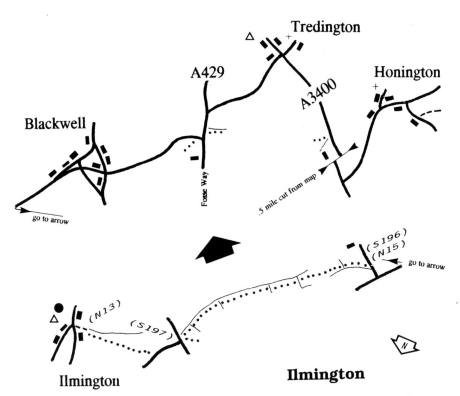

Blackwell

A429

Tredington

Honington

Fosse Way

.5 mile cut from map

go to arrow

go to arrow

(S196)
(N15)

(N13)

(S197)

Ilmington

Ilmington

(N12) From phone box opposite Howard Arms, face pub & go R to road junction. Take track opposite, pass cottage & shed & take gap R into field.

(N13) Bear R midway between farthest power pole & L hedge. When in view, head for middle (unguyed) power pole & KEEP SAME LINE down to hedge gap & lane. Go L to T junction & cross stile opposite.

see note re
ALTERNATIVE
◀ *page 112*
Alternative (N13a)
Official route (N14)

(119)

Ilmington

(S198) Face Howard Arms & go L. Pass shop & follow tarmac path (past Manor House) to big thatched cottage (The Bevingtons).

(S199) Go R to churchyard. Go L round church to lane. Go L 50yds to junction (by Hurdle Maker) & go R to end of lane.

(S200) Go ahead on green track & take gate. Go on 25yds & cross corner stile R. Go R by hedge & cross corner stile.

(S201) Go half L past midfield markpost to power pole & cross corner stile. Go ahead, bear L to pass pool on your R [Newfound-land Well] & climb to cross corner stile.

(S202) Go L on fenced track (via stile) & take gate/stile. Bear L to valley bottom & cross stile.

(S203) Go R by stream & cross next stile. Go L round field edge & up to join drive. Go R to lane, then R down to road. ▶

(N7) Follow 200yds & take drive L. Follow 100yds & step L onto field. Go down with fence on your R, round field corner & cross stile R.

(N8) Go L by stream & cross next stile. Go half R up hillside & take gate/stile. Follow fenced track 250yds (via stile) to crest, & cross stile R.

(N9) Go half L down to pool [Newfoundland Well] Climb to power pole & cross L of 2 stiles. Cross field diagonally to markpost & bear R to cross midhedge stile.

(N10) Follow L hedge & cross corner stile. Go ahead 5 paces then L past big holly to take gate. Go ahead & join lane to road junction (by Hurdle Maker).

(N11) Go L 50 yds & enter churchyard. Follow path round church (past 1st corner & path R) to corner by field. Go L to big thatched cottage. Go L past Manor House & shop to Howard Arms at

Ilmington
◀

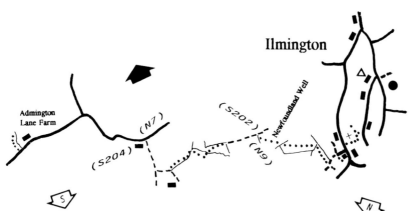

Ilmington

(S204) Go L .6 mile (past lane R) to just past Admington Lane Farm, & cross stile R.

(N6) Go L .6 mile (past lane L) to pass Larkstoke Cottage & take lane R.

Ilmington

(S205) Follow R hedge/ trees round 1st bend to 90deg corner. Go half L to projecting hedge corner

(S206) Go L by hedge & round field corner plus 85 yds to cross footbridge L.

(S207) Take gap L & go R by hedge to cross corner hurdle/stile thing. Go up half R & cross stile L of bungalow to lane.

(S208) Go R 50yds & take drive L. [Meon Hall] Pass barn plus 50 yds & cross gate/stile R. Bear L & take gate/stile.

(S209) Cross summit ahead to projecting hedge corner, then go with hedge on your R to cross stile & plank. Go R & cross corner stiles & plank.

(S210) Go L by hedge & cross corner stile. Go half R to cross bottom corner stile. ►

(N2) Go L past front doors & follow fenced path to stile & paddock. Cross stile ahead, go R by fence & cross stile. Go to top L field corner & cross stile.

(N3) Follow R hedge to corner, cross stiles & plank R. Go ahead a few paces to cross plank & stile L. Follow L hedge to its corner, then keep same line over summit to gates /stiles & drive. [Meon Hall]

(N4) Go L to lane. Go R 50 yds past bungalow & cross stile L. Go down field diagonally & cross hurdle/ stile thingy. Follow L hedge to corner & take gap L.

(N5) Go R & cross foot-bridge. Go R, round field corner & follow hedge up to corner. Turn half R to nearest end of LIGHT green conifers. Go with trees on your L to stile & road. [Admington Lane Farm] ◄

(S211) Follow L fence by paddock & cross stile L. Go ahead, cross stile, follow fenced path to road & go R to green at

Upper Quinton

Upper Quinton

(N1) Start with a ritual sit on Centenary Way seat, then get up & go half R to road by phone pole. Go R 200yds to white Meon Cottage L.

◄

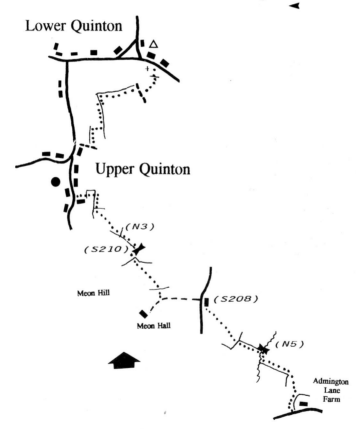

(123)

Church of St John the Baptist, Brinklow

(124)